Becoming Your Spouse's Better Half

Why Differences Make a Marriage Great

RICK JOHNSON

Revell
a division of Baker Publishing Group
Grand Rapids, Michigan

© 2010 by Rick Johnson

Published by Revell
a division of Baker Publishing Group
P.O. Box 6287, Grand Rapids, MI 49516-6287
www.revellbooks.com

Printed in the United States of America

Library of Congress Cataloging-in-Publication Data
Johnson, Rick, 1956–
    Becoming your spouse's better half : why differences make a marriage great / Rick Johnson.
      p. cm.
    Includes bibliographical references.
    ISBN 978-0-8007-3250-9 (pbk.)
    1. Marriage—Religious aspects—Christianity. 2. Sex differences—Religious aspects—Christianity. I. Title.
    BV835.J63 2010
    248.8′44—dc22
                                                       2009034666

Published in association with the literary agency of WordServe Literary Group, Ltd., 10152 S. Knoll Circle, Highlands Ranch, CO 80130.

10   11   12   13   14   15   16   7   6   5   4   3   2   1

This book is dedicated to Scott and Terry for the model they set and for their encouragement. Also to Dick and Dot for their love and example.

And of course, to the love of my life, the woman who taught me to love—my "till death do us part" bride, Suzanne. You'll always be my girl.

Contents

Contents

Acknowledgments

I would like to thank Greg and Becky Johnson for the initial idea of and their invaluable help with this book.

Also, I'd like to thank my editor Dr. Vicki Crumpton, who is (surprisingly) not tired of working with me yet. I also would like to acknowledge all the people at my publisher who work so hard behind the scenes to produce and sell my books. I truly believe God gave me the best publishing house and the best people I could ever want to work with—thank you!

I'd also like to thank the many women who responded to my questionnaires while I was trying to understand how women think and what they need. (I've changed their names to protect their privacy.) Your patience and honesty were invaluable as I searched for a glimpse inside the complicated soul of the female gender.

Ceasing to be "in love" need not mean ceasing to love. Love in this second sense—love as distinct from "being in love"—is not merely a feeling. It is a deep unity, maintained by the will and deliberately strengthened by habit; reinforced by (in Christian marriages) the grace which both partners ask, and receive, from God. . . . "Being in love" first moved them to promise fidelity: this quieter love enables them to keep the promise. It is on this love that the engine of marriage is run: being in love was the explosion that started it.

C. S. Lewis, *Mere Christianity*

Introduction

Marriage Is Tough

Marriage is tough. Anyone who says it isn't is either a liar or a fool. Even after twenty-eight years of marriage, trying to understand and satisfy my wife's needs is still a daunting challenge. And I'm sure she feels the same way about me.

It's not that we don't have great times together. In fact, we're best friends. I enjoy her company as much or more than I ever have. My respect for her has grown exponentially over the years. Over time the initial rush of heart-stopping passion, lust, and infatuation has been replaced by a more mature, steady, deeper love and affection. I still find her the most beautiful and mysterious creature I've ever known.

Sometimes I look at an attractive woman and then look at my wife. I am always astonished at how beautiful she still is, even in comparison to much younger women. She's charming, and her emerald green eyes sparkle with electricity when she's being flirtatious. Every so often I look at her and am stunned speechless when I see a vision of the young girl I married who has ripened into an even more glorious version of womanhood. When she laughs at my jokes, all is good with the world. Her peals of laughter warm my insides like a cup of hot cocoa on a frosty winter's day. Our bodies fit together like a pair of comfortable old Levi's. She truly is what makes my world go around.

Differences—Strengths or Weaknesses?

Despite all that, we are two separate beings with individual backgrounds, tastes, experiences, and personalities. This merger of individual identities is the confluence that blends two separate streams of consciousness into the river of marriage. Even though I respect and admire her more than anyone I've ever met, she still frequently frustrates me to the point of exasperation. She is a bewildering mix of quandaries, enigmas, contradictions, and vexations. And I'm no better. We are two unique individuals with opposing personalities and habits.

One glaring example would be the time we spend in the bathroom. I typically shower, shave, and slap on some Old Spice, and I'm good to go. Give me another minute or so to slip on jeans and a T-shirt, and I'm ready—a total of ten minutes tops (fifteen if I'm taking my time) from start to finish. Suzanne, however, uses a considerably greater amount of time and resources preparing for the day. I've never actually timed her with a stopwatch, but I'm pretty sure that even under times of great urgency, she's never broken the one-hour barrier. And that definitely does not include getting dressed. Of course, the end result is a whole lot more spectacular than how I turn out, but the amount of time spent seems a little excessive to me.

In almost everything, we are diametrically opposed. For instance, I can guarantee that anywhere we go in the world, the absolute strangest person in the room will come up and talk to her. She draws those people like a magnet. Then she enjoys spending time chatting with the "different" kinds of people who approach her. Perhaps that is what makes her such a great special-needs teacher. I, on the other hand, tend to try to discourage those kinds of individuals from latching on to me. Frankly, they make me a little nervous.

In addition, Suzanne is bizarrely unorganized; I like to know where everything is. She is incorrigibly late; I believe anything less than five minutes early is disrespectful. She likes vegetables; I like meat. She is very relatable in one-on-one situations; I teach well in front of large groups. She is more loving and intuitive; I am more analytical and logical. She is flexible to change and comfortable in the face of surprises (in fact, she appears to relish chaos); I need to be prepared and organized in order to be comfortable.

However, because we have recognized the value of these differences, we are able to use our strengths to compensate for and even complement the other's weaknesses. It makes us a formidable team, both in ministry and in our marriage. We believe that as a team we are greater than the sum of our parts. While her differences may annoy me from time to time, I have come to understand the value they bring to our relationship. We have worked out our roles in marriage so they are complementary, allowing us to thrive by working together instead of against one another.

This doesn't mean that we are not equal partners, or that one is more dominant than another. Equality in a relationship does not mean sameness—it means each person is valued for the contribution they bring to the table. In fact, the very differences we have are perhaps our greatest strengths when they are recognized and used effectively instead of being at odds with one another.

Why You Chose Who You Chose

Did you ever wonder why you were attracted to the person you were, and why they were attracted to you? Not only that, but remember how exciting it was when you first met your spouse-to-be? Life was fun and you felt alive! What was that all about?

Harville Hendrix, in his classic book *Getting the Love You Want*, explains what happens during the attraction phase of a relationship:

> The brain releases dopamine and norepinephrine, two of the body's many neurotransmitters. These neurotransmitters help contribute to a rosy outlook on life, a rapid pulse, increased energy, and a sense of heightened perception. During this phase, when lovers want to be together every moment of the day, the brain increases its production of endorphins and enkephalins, natural narcotics, enhancing a person's sense of security and comfort.[1]

Most lovers report going through phases where they feel that they have always known the other person (even when having just met), that the other person is easy to talk to, and that they couldn't live without that person. Hendrix purports that when we meet someone having negative characteristics that remind us of our parents or childhood caretakers, a portion of our brain is unconsciously and instinctively attracted to that person as a way of trying to "go back" and meet certain basic needs that were not fulfilled during childhood. The unconscious mind is trying to repair our wounds

14

by attracting us to people who have the same compilation of bad characteristics as those who wounded us in childhood.

One reason we feel so good at the beginning of a relationship is that part of our brain believes we have finally been given a chance to be nurtured and become whole again—the way God created us. This may work out great, or it may result in disaster, as neither we nor our mate are conscious of this desire to get these needs met. The greater the damage done during childhood, the needier and more dramatic our desire for fulfillment becomes. And since our mate is not the offending parent, he or she will probably not be able to fill that void left over from childhood.

During courtship, this unconscious drive in our brain frequently causes us to be in denial regarding many of the negative traits of our mate-to-be. Because that need for wholeness is so powerful, we are tempted to overlook or even deny the existence of characteristics that later on tend to annoy us. They seemed cute at the time but drive us crazy once the bloom of romance has worn thin.

Additionally, have you ever noticed that most people marry someone with the opposite qualities and characteristics they have? For instance, if someone is introverted, he or she generally marries a person who is an extrovert. Someone who is messy frequently marries a person who is highly organized. This is because during childhood, certain traits or facets of our psyche and personality are unhealthily repressed, denied, or lost, creating a false self-image or at least a partial psyche that we present to the world and even to ourselves. So when we meet someone who possesses those traits we have repressed or lost, we are naturally drawn to them as a way of vicariously attempting to regain our wholeness. We feel comfortable, for that person's strengths round out our being, and thus we are drawn to them.

Realizing this can benefit both partners and the relationship. The problem comes when both partners expect and need the other to fix their needs, but neither knows what those needs are or how to meet them.[2]

But a healthy marriage can heal our wounds and help bring us to wholeness. Drs. Les and Leslie Parrott say, "Wholeness is found in an *interdependent* relationship, in which two people with self-respect and dignity make a commitment to nurture his or her own spiritual growth, as well as his or her partner's."[3]

Why Marriages Falter

Marriage today seems less binding than a cell phone contract. The average first marriage in this country lasts seven years. The average second marriage lasts five. As if the challenges of a first marriage weren't tough enough, anyone who has been in a blended family will tell you about the myriad of additional trials this scenario presents: two sets of kids; two separate histories; two completely different life philosophies, parenting styles, and sets of baggage. And when two sets of careers and monies are mixed in along with the obligatory prenuptial agreements, it's almost like admitting that the marriage is doomed to fail anyway.

Because of the legacy they've observed from their parents' generation, most young people today are fairly pessimistic about the chances of a marriage lasting a lifetime. If you talk to them about marriage, you can see that they yearn for the kind of intimacy possible only through a long-lasting relationship, but they have little hope of having one themselves. Couples may spend hundreds of hours and tens of thousands of dollars on the actual wedding day, but no energy, resources, or forethought whatsoever toward the marriage that follows.

Many people quickly discover that being married and staying in love are just plain hard work—too hard. Combine that intense struggle with our society's instant-gratification mantra, the court's "no fault" divorce laws, and a cultural legacy of relative truth, and you have a recipe for divorce. Our Western culture does not like to suffer, so we shy away from anything that is uncomfortable or difficult. When marriage is tough, many people just think it's broken and then go look for another mate who won't be so much work.

Unfortunately, the problem is generally with us and therefore follows us from relationship to relationship. I recently told a friend that a first divorce we might be able to blame on our partner, but any divorces after that we need to look in the mirror to see where the problem lies. And one fact that almost no one wants to admit is that the person we fell in love with is at the same level of emotional maturity we are. Look at your spouse and know that they are probably just as emotionally mature as you are, all your protests notwithstanding.

Also, the expectations each partner brings into a relationship make a huge difference in how successful that marriage will be. Unrealistic expectations that cannot be met by either spouse can make both partners miserable. Discussing numerous relevant topics such as religious expectations, number of children, parenting styles, familial obligations toward extended family, sexual expectations, and the roles and duties of each spouse (to name just a few) *before* entering into marriage is a crucial factor to preventing problems later on.

So, if God ordained marriage as the way a man and woman should live together as one flesh, then there must be some way he designed that to happen. What guidelines did he provide to help us understand how to keep from killing each other or, even worse, creating families just to turn around and tear them asunder? What types of things do couples who have been married for a long time say are important, and what advice do they give to create longevity in a marriage?

In my research for this book, I discovered that men frequently operate on an objective-based, goal-oriented system, while women more often incorporate a whole-world view in their thematic approach to life. These observations can best be summed up as a husband's "seven modes" and a wife's "seven moods."

Guys tend to operate in modes, which allows them to compartmentalize the different areas of their life; women tend to be driven by moods or emotions. Males are able to separate the various components of their life and forget about some while concentrating on others. Seldom does one area of life bleed into the others. Women, on the other hand, tend to view life as an overall "whole" with every area of their lives interconnected and interrelated. These differences alone are baffling and often confusing to the opposite gender. Bill and Pam Farrel describe this as women thinking like a pot of spaghetti, where everything touches everything else, and men thinking like waffles, where each element of their life is in a separate box.[4] Helen Fisher, in her book *The First Sex*, says women tend to think in terms of "interrelated factors, not straight lines," whereas men use "compartmentalized, incremental reasoning process."[5]

When a husband understands and appreciates his wife's moods, and when a wife recognizes and respects her husband's modes of operation, marriage becomes a wonder instead of work, fascinating instead of frustrating, a commitment to intimacy instead of a settling for "just staying together."

People want an easy marriage. They don't want love to be so much work. Two people start out with their hearts melting as one in a natural way, but they're living on the high of bliss-filled hormones. This will carry them for a while, but people can't live on bliss; there will always be a "coming down," or crash, from the high. When that happens, and they are un-prepared for the daily labor of love, they will soon be hitting their heads against the walls of each other's hearts.

When we're willing to put forth the effort to understand our mates and help our mates understand us, this softens our hearts and opens the door to intimacy. When we don't make this effort together, usually one partner will stop banging his or her head against the wall of the other's heart and give up. While fighting can be a red flag, a relationship reaches a critical stage when one spouse or the other stops trying and gives up.

When you have the key, it's easy to go in and out. You don't have to knock the door down or break a window. You just walk in. But without the key to understanding, marriage is hard work.

Ideally, a Christian marriage begins with both parties committed to loving God and each other. But later, after the "buzz" of love begins to fizzle, communication tails off and spouses can start taking each other for granted, losing empathy, respect, and love for one another. Life is tough, and instead of working as a team, they begin fighting with each other in an attempt to get their individual needs met. They scream at and accuse their mates and then expect their mates to want to satisfy their needs. Each spouse soon loses the desire to meet the other's needs, and each loses sight of the fact that love is an action, not an emotion. That is why the very action of meeting the other's needs (acting loving) can lead to feeling the emotion of love. Without that action, it is natural to slide into a state of need and self-indulgent gratification.

Harville Hendrix explains this mentality:

Their partners are going to do it all—satisfy unmet childhood needs, complement lost self-parts, nurture them in a
consistent and loving way, and be eternally available to them.
These are the same expectations that fueled the excitement
of romantic love, but now there is less of a desire to reciprocate. After all, people don't get married to take care of their
partners' needs—they get married to further their own psychological and emotional growth. Once a relationship seems
secure, a psychological switch is triggered deep in the old
brain that activates all the latent infantile wishes.[6]

Eventually, husbands and wives allow their neediness—
their lack of understanding, empathy, and respect for each
other—to pull them away, instead of using their differences
to glue them together. If lack of understanding and loss of
respect happens over a span of years, the intimacy that could
have been created through a couple's differences becomes a
chasm that is often too wide to bring them together again
as one flesh.

A chain reaction or vicious circle is the inevitable result:
Lack of understanding and respect lead to hurt, confusion,
anger, and frustration, which lead to contempt, hate, or resig-
nation. Those feelings then lead to physical escape (oftentimes sinful behavior) and/or emotional divorce, with the
appearance of marriage but not the intimacy, and finally end
in legal divorce, with all of the ramifications that this has to
future generations.

Anyone who has been through a divorce will tell you what
a painful, gut-wrenching experience it is. And we are only
just now recognizing the devastating effects to children whose
families have been ripped apart. Perhaps now is the time to
start trying to understand how to turn all marriages, good or

struggling, into a satisfying lifelong commitment. Previous generations did it. Why do we struggle so much?

How to Use This Book

This book has chapters for men and chapters for women. It was meant to be read together by a husband and wife. The "Men's Modes" section is to enlighten women about their husbands, and the "Women's Moods" section is to help men understand their wives' needs.

My wife and I love reading books together. Every evening we try to sit down and pray together before reading a portion of a book. Generally I read out loud to her while she knits or does some other repetitive task. Other times she reads aloud while I am fixing something that doesn't require much concentration. This activity has allowed us to grow together, and it helps us spend quality time together each day. It also creates great intimacy between us and prompts us to have quality discussions about important topics that we might never have talked about. However, this takes a significant amount of effort and commitment on the part of both spouses. It is very easy to take a day off and then never get back into it again. But I have noticed that when we as a couple are consistently praying and reading together, our relationship and marriage are at peak performance.

This book has two sections—one for women and one for men—each with seven chapters. The chapters on women's moods should help men understand their wives better. Likewise, as women read the chapters on men's modes, I hope they'll understand their husbands better.

Since women are generally more relationally minded, I wanted the men to feel understood and inspired at the start. Guys, if you're anything like me, I was afraid if you were forced to read through seven chapters of women's needs first, you might get bored, frustrated, or just plain overwhelmed and want to quit, so I began with men's modes.

Reading the chapters together will allow both of you to stop and ask questions as they come up. It's a good chance to determine whether you think I'm full of baloney or whether I'm making some good points that can transform your relationship. Ideally, both husband and wife will understand how the other gender functions and operates, making for a better relationship and marriage.

Expectations

I've now lived more years as an adult with my wife than I lived before I got married. We've raised two babies to adulthood together, suffered through a business failure, been rich and been poor (more often poor), and helped each other through devastating personal losses. My relationship with my wife today is changing rapidly just by the nature of our ministry's growth and the challenges that presents. We also just launched our children into the world. We need to be on the same page and understand what makes each other tick in order to grow together and weather the storms we face caused by these changes. We need to grow together, not apart, to have a successful marriage in times of change and the stresses that brings.

Your marriage relationship is a living, dynamic entity. It needs continuous nurturing, refining, changing, and fine-tuning. Hendrix describes marriage this way:

> Marriage is a psychological and spiritual journey that begins with the ecstasy of attraction, meanders through a rocky stretch of self-discovery, and culminates in the creation of an

intimate, joyful, lifelong union. Whether or not you realize the full potential of this vision depends not on your ability to attract the perfect mate, but on your willingness to acquire knowledge about hidden parts of yourself.[7]

Marriages that do not last long enough to go through the rocky stretches of self-discovery never reach that destination of an intimate, joyful, lifelong union that Hendrix talks about. This requires sacrifice on your part. Your mate is not perfect, and the truth is the only person you can change is yourself. Your relationship will change as each of you grows and enters into new seasons of life. After all, the only constant in life is change.

This book will help you and your spouse understand each other better. Simply recognizing that men and women are pretty much diametrically opposite can help you relate to and accept your spouse. Then when you understand how and why someone does something, it allows you to develop empathy for them, which helps you to see things from that person's perspective. When that happens, love and intimacy soon follow, and they will give you the ability to have a fun, healthy, lifelong marriage.

I encourage you to read this book with the expectation that it will change your marriage and help draw you closer to your spouse. The expectations with which we enter into something generally greatly increase the odds of those goals being fulfilled. Your marriage is too important not to believe with all your heart that it can be a loving, dynamic, lifelong experience.

So get ready, because you are about to experience the awesome process of growing together and becoming lifelong partners in this frightfully wonderful relationship God created called marriage. Hang on, because it can be a bumpy but ultimately incredibly satisfying journey.

Men's Modes

> Satisfaction in individual love cannot be attained
> without the capacity to love one's neighbor, with-
> out true humility, courage, faith and discipline. In
> a culture in which these qualities are rare, the at-
> tainment of the capacity of love must remain a rare
> achievement.
>
> Erich Fromm, *The Art of Loving*

Women have an incredible power to influence their husbands. Much like God has given men great power
to impact people's lives for generations by the things they
do or don't do today, women too have been endowed with a
more subtle but equally effective and powerful influence. This
influence allows them to encourage and inspire their men to
attempt and accomplish things they would never be able to
without a woman by their side.

In the movie *The African Queen*, Rosie (Katharine Hep-
burn), a middle-aged spinster missionary, uses her consider-

able feminine charm and guile to convince Charlie (Humphrey Bogart), an unambitious, gin-soaked riverboat captain, to attempt impossible challenges he does not want to try and does not feel adequate to perform. She cajoles, maneuvers, and finally convinces him that he is able to achieve things that few men could do. He feels compelled to try and then actually accomplishes challenges like navigating a wild jungle river; straightening a twisted axle by building a primitive smelter; manufacturing a fin and welding it onto the broken boat propeller; and finally designing and producing torpedoes from scrap materials to turn their boat into a floating bomb, in order to blow up a German patrol boat.

In my book *The Man Whisperer*, I talk about this power that a woman has to encourage her man to greatness or to actually destroy him, sometimes merely with a few words or even just a look. A woman has this great power for a very simple reason. Most men have a hard shell they show to the world that protects their vulnerable ego. This ego is vulnerable because most men secretly feel inadequate. They seldom drop this shield and allow anyone inside their defenses.

The one person in the whole world to whom a man drops this defensive shield, if only occasionally, is his wife. Because she knows the "true" man (not the face he shows the world), this gives a woman great power to encourage or to devastate a man with her words and actions. It's one of the reasons a wife's respect is so important to a man. If his wife—who knows him better than anyone else, who has looked at all those secret places in his heart—doesn't respect him, how can anyone else respect him? How can he respect himself?

The woman who understands that power and then recognizes that a man operates throughout his life differently than a woman—that his life is governed by modes, not moods— has a wonderful gift in the palm of her hand. She can use her

God-given abilities to nurture an intimate relationship with her spouse while using her strengths to bolster and compensate for his weaknesses as part of a committed team. When that happens, a healthy, loving, long-term relationship can flourish.

The following modes are ones that most men experience throughout life. They are compartments of a man's life containing important needs that must be met in order for him to lead a productive life and experience a healthy relationship. Unlike women, men's needs are pretty simple and straightforward. Figure out a way to meet these needs, and most men will be happy and contented. Not only that, but they will be more able and much more willing to fall all over themselves to meet their woman's needs.

Amorous

Never Give Up!

> Regina was washing her face in the master bath-
> room when Ramone came up and undressed for bed.
> He noticed her outfit, one of Diego's football team
> T-shirts and worn pajama bottoms, and read the
> message: no sex tonight. But he was a man, as dim
> and hopeful as any other. He wasn't going to let
> some dowdy old outfit stop him completely. He'd
> give it a try.
>
> George Pelecanos, *The Night Gardener*

I like dogs. Dogs are ever optimistic, always hopeful that a meaty bone or a good belly rub is just around the corner. Much like their animal best friends, husbands too are always optimistic, hoping—sometimes against all odds—that a good bout of sex will be just around the corner.

Why do men place so much significance on this physical act that many women look at as either a fun activity (if the time is right) or an unpleasant duty (if the timing isn't right)? Since sex may be *the* most important need in a man's life, we begin the book with this topic. Most women do not truly understand this need, so let's look at what men think and why sex is so important to a man's life.

How Men View Sex

From a sexual perspective, men tend to view women as objects. That sounds horrible and is something that radical feminists have been using against men for years. But men have the capability to compartmentalize the areas of their lives, especially in the sexual arena. This ability to compartmentalize is why a man can have sex even if he's been arguing with his wife.

In fact, many men feel sex actually solves the other problems of life. It is also one of the reasons why even good men who understand that the girls in pornography are victims are still able to look at them. We hear about men who are pillars of the community and should know better getting caught having flings with women who are not their wives or even with underage prostitutes.

Why would these men risk their families, careers, and even their lives engaging in these kinds of sexual peccadilloes? It is because they are able to separate those activities from other areas of their lives and so are more easily able to justify them in their minds. And as self-righteous or prideful as many of us would like to profess being about this topic, none of us men are immune to falling into this trap. It is something we must continually, even obsessively, be on guard about. Given the right time and circumstances, any man is prey to fall into sexual sin.

Every man struggles with lust, but it has nothing to do with his wife. It is an issue that a man struggles with inside himself. It is a battle between the factions of his soul. It is not due to anything his wife does or doesn't do, the way she looks, how much she weighs, or how adept she is at satisfying him sexually. Understand that all men struggle with lust to one degree or another. Even men who are married to Victoria's Secret models lust for other women. A man learns to control this impulse partly as a function of the amount of respect he has for a woman, but it still lurks in the background of his consciousness. It is unrealistic to think that a man will never struggle with this issue, regardless of how much he loves his wife.

Women often seem shocked when good men fall in this arena, but men know that they are weak and that the constant onslaught of sexually graphic images they are subjected to on a daily basis has the capability of wearing them down. Society's casual approach to sexual morality has created a huge divot in the ability of both men and women to remain faithful to their wedding vows. It is estimated that 60 percent of men and 40 percent of women engage in extramarital affairs.[1] In about 41 percent of marriages, one or the other partner is unfaithful.[2]

Most younger adults do not understand that our culture has changed dramatically in the past thirty years. Behaviors that were unthinkable just a few years ago are commonplace today. Easy access to Internet pornography and the sexualization of our society have lured many men and women into situations they would never have expected and have encouraged many others to loosen their moral compass. The steady erosion of personal values has opened the door to the slippery slope of cultural corrosion.

Men also tend to become less interested sexually in their wives after having children or seeing their wives give birth, as they view them as more maternal than sexual. And after years of marriage, sex can become routine and mechanical, causing men to seek that rush of adrenaline and excitement that was present during the "chase and conquer" phase of the relationship. The acceptability of provocative and revealing clothing, readily accessible pornography, and women eager to meet men under the cloak of anonymity on the Internet only exacerbate the struggle for men to remain sexually pure.

Higher levels of the hormone testosterone and its effects on the male body and psyche create a much higher sex drive in men than in women. God created men like this to perpetuate the species. If you only knew how difficult it is for a man to avert his eyes when he walks past a beautiful woman on the street, you'd appreciate him that much more.

I'm sure it's not a surprise to you that men and women think about sex differently and have different needs in this area. It's easy to acknowledge those differences in general. But couples who do not recognize that these differences apply to their *own* relationship or who bring their personal baggage into the relationship can find themselves stunned by what happens. Personal baggage might include anything ranging from childhood wounds, sexual abuse, or previous broken relationships to relationship preconceptions and role stereotypes from childhood. Dr. William Glasser describes this scenario:

> In the beginning of a marriage, many partners, especially women, are fooled by sex into believing that the men love them more than they actually do. This is because for women, unlike men, sex is more genetically tied to their need for love than to their need to survive. A man with a strong survival need wants a lot of sex and, in the beginning, acts loving to get it.
>
> But as the marriage continues, the woman usually sees through this act and realizes that the man loves sex as much

or more than he loves her, and she becomes less interested in this hormonal, less loving act. As she loses interest, the man becomes more frustrated and demands more sex, which turns her off further, and the marriage deteriorates. . . .

A woman with a very strong need for love recognizes that her partner needs less love, and she is attracted, even challenged, by this difference. Driven by her strong need for love, she believes she will be able to love him so much that her love will bring out a latent need she is sure is there. Sometimes she succeeds, literally teaches him to love more. But in most cases, if she is too insistent and tries too hard, she fails.[3]

For women, especially those with a powerful need to be loved, these differences in how men look at sex versus how women perceive it can be devastating.

Men think about sex all the time—even in the most inappropriate of places such as in church or at funerals. They can be stimulated by nothing—for no reason at all. They can become aroused purely as a physical function of their gender.

Just like women have a monthly cycle, men also have a cycle. The human male, because of sperm production and other factors, naturally desires sexual release about every forty-eight to seventy-two hours.[4] That's every two to three days! (My wife accuses me of having made up this statistic.) One woman calls her husband "Mr. Predictable" because of his every third day "resurrection."

Study your husband to determine his "cycle." You'll notice that generally the day after having had his sexual needs met, he will be calmer, nicer, and generally more able to pay attention to details. He also probably won't be very attentive to you. But by the third day (or longer) he should start focusing more on you. He enjoys that focus, and part of the thrill of the hunt for a man is chasing you until he catches you. This is a normal pattern in a man to focus more on his wife as his need for physical fulfillment increases.

Our friend Brenda was mentoring a young married woman. One day the young woman came to her in tears, explaining that her husband only seemed to be interested in her *before* having sex and that after, he didn't pay any attention to her. That behavior hurt her feelings and made her feel like she was being used. Because Brenda had been married for a while and was used to the ways of her husband, she gently explained to the distraught young wife that if she just looked at the situation in a different light, it would make all the difference in the world.

Brenda explained that by meeting her husband's physical needs, she was filling his tank, so to speak. Once his needs were met, he was willing and able to go out and conquer the world. The truth is he was not capable of focusing on the details of life and work when preoccupied with sexual desire. That programming, with its urgent need, overrides all other operating systems. Brenda explained that men tend to refocus on details after getting their sexual needs met, and that when a wife meets her husband's sexual needs, she helps him better face the world just as if she was providing him with food, love, or any other physical or emotional nourishment.

That advice sounds better coming from a woman than a man, but it doesn't make it any less true. That being said, men must also recognize the need that women have to be held a little longer and be lingered over after romance is complete.

A newlywed youth pastor's wife asked another pastor's wife, who had been married for many years, for advice in being married to a pastor. The older woman mentored the younger woman by telling her that her main job as the wife of a pastor was to have sex with her husband. She explained it by saying that all of his other needs could be met by someone else, but having sex was the only need that couldn't (and shouldn't) be met by anyone else.

I about coughed my Coke through my nose when she told that story, but this is clearly a woman of wisdom and maturity. She understood that she plays a big role in fulfilling this most basic need of her husband. (Somehow, though, I doubt if that is taught in Ministry 101 classes at seminary school.)

With that in mind, what kinds of activities are appealing to a man in this area?

What Motivates Him

Let's be open and honest in this section on sex. Unfortunately, my editor won't let me go into graphic detail for fear that some elderly lady in a Christian bookstore in Cleghorn, Iowa, will be shocked into a dead faint. But I'll at least give you a few perspectives from a male's point of view on what makes for a fulfilling sex life. Understand that these are generalities and that not all men are the same. But I think these general guidelines will help any woman understand how to satisfy this area of her man's life.

If you are newlyweds reading this book, or even young couples in your twenties, understand that you probably don't need to know some of this stuff. Your husband has a constantly charged battery that keeps his motor humming and ready for action, so to speak. Unless he's under a great amount of stress at work or in other areas of life, all you need to do is be available and he'll be happy. For the rest of you, here goes.

First of all, recognize that men are very visual, so we are stimulated and excited by what we see. What excites us more than anything is seeing a woman's body. That's why pornography, nude magazines, and strip clubs are so popular. Contrary to what we might claim, we don't buy *Penthouse* magazine for the jokes or interesting articles. Your womanly body is extremely exciting to your husband, and he wants to see it. That doesn't mean you need to parade around naked all the time (although . . .), but a little suggestive glimpse every now and again rapidly raises a man's blood pressure. In fact, oftentimes less is more. A flash of thigh or a quick glimpse down an open top are generally more invigorating than complete nudity. And even if you're covered, the thought of what you might *not* be wearing is also very enticing.

However, because men spent thousands of years as hunters, their other senses, such as smell and sound, are highly attuned to stimulate them as well. The sounds of lovemaking are very arousing to a man, so if you like something, let him know—maybe even loudly. If you've ever watched the movie *When Harry Met Sally*, you know that one of the more attention-attracting sounds in the universe for a guy is a female experiencing sexual pleasure.

Smells are an intoxicating spice to a male as well. Even boys fall under the spell of a woman's perfume. In his book *The Greatest Thing Since Sliced Bread*, Don Robertson's eight-year-old protagonist, Morris Bird III, describes his attractive teacher this way: "He smelled her perfume. It was always the same perfume, and it put him in mind of grass on a warm day after the rain. It was a very green smell, but in no way did it knock you down. Instead, it made your breath feel good, and Morris Bird III for one was never happier than when his breath felt good."[5]

But most of all, for a man, sex begins inside his head. A man's mind and imagination drive his sexuality. A man usually doesn't have affairs because of lust but because of boredom. That need for something different and exciting stimulates his sexual psyche. Doing the same thing sexually, the same way, the same time of day, in the same position can become very boring to a man over time. A little creativity in the bedroom (or any other room) goes a long way toward fulfilling this need in a man. The saying "variety is the spice of life" may well have been spoken first about sex.

Perhaps being created to procreate and populate the world fuels this masculine drive to mate in a variety of circumstances and with different people. I am not promoting promiscuity, but it does explain this craving in most men. Good men control that powerful drive because they realize doing so is in the best interest of their wives, their children, themselves, and society (not to mention being obedient to God's law).

What is acceptable in the area of sexual relations between a husband and wife who are Christians? Sex isn't something discussed very much in the average church (or even by your parents). I would say that anything that is mutually satisfactory and doesn't cause emotional, psychological, or physical pain to a husband and wife is fair game in the bedroom, as long as it doesn't cause either party to enter into sin. Obviously it cannot involve other people either physically or mentally (such as using pornography). Role playing, game playing, dress up, creative positions, and new locations all seem pretty harmless when performed between consenting spouses. It is one of the reasons why a hotel stay is usually pretty invigorating to a married couple's sex drive. That spice of change and risk adds a certain element of adventure and even perception of danger to the act.

I know that most women probably think dressing up in costumes or little frilly negligees with heels is somewhat silly. But remember that men are very visual creatures. After all, they're not attracted to look at sexy photographs because their hearing is so acute. The imagination is the greatest aphrodisiac, so a little role playing with costumes can really spice things up every once in a while.

Want to get his motor humming? Call him up at work and whisper naughty things to him. (Just make sure he's not on a speakerphone.) Or sneak a risqué note in his lunch when he doesn't expect it. He'll probably be home early from work on those days, so you better have the kids over at a neighbor's that afternoon.

God certainly recognizes the importance sex plays in a marriage relationship. This verse spells it out pretty plainly:

> Let the husband render to his wife the affection due her, and likewise also the wife to her husband. The wife does not have authority over her own body, but the husband does. And likewise the husband does not have authority over his own body, but the wife does. Do not deprive one another except with consent for a time, that you may give yourselves to fasting and prayer; and come together again so that Satan does not tempt you because of your lack of self-control.
>
> 1 Corinthians 7:3–5

This passage speaks frankly to the fact that married couples should have normal, healthy sexual relations—that depriving either partner of their natural rights in this area may be conducive to temptation or sexual immorality. Both husband and wife have conjugal privileges and exclusive possession of the other in this area. The biggest challenge for most men is to not say or do something stupid to make the wife mad after she reveals she will be "in the mood" that night.

When a woman looks at sex from her husband's perspective and recognizes its importance to him, she can begin to use it as a tool to better their relationship.

His Needs

While sex is a powerful *physical* need for a man, it is much more than that. Sex also fulfills a powerful *emotional* need. Author Shaunti Feldhahn says, "Lack of sex is as emotionally serious to him as, say, his sudden silence would be to you, were he simply to stop communicating with you. It is just as wounding to him, just as much a legitimate grievance—and just as dangerous to your marriage."[6]

Sex for a man really is not optional, as many women believe. Feldhahn continues, "In a very deep way, your man often feels isolated and burdened by secret feelings of inadequacy. Making love with you assures him that you find him desirable, salves a deep sense of loneliness, and gives him the strength and well-being necessary to face the world with confidence. And, of course, sex also makes him feel loved—in fact, he can't feel completely loved without it."[7]

While men psychologically, emotionally, and physically need regular sex, it is important to remember that a man would rather have less sex with a willing partner than more sex with a woman who considers it a "duty." So, if you as the wife have the attitude of, "Okay, let's get it over with," he might not turn it down, but it will not be very satisfying to him. When you desire him physically, you have the power to salve many of the wounds this world inflicts upon him. A man who is desired by his wife meets the world with confidence and enthusiasm. One of a man's most basic needs is to feel wanted physically by a woman. When a man feels that his wife desires him, it gives him a big boost of self-confidence.

Your husband needs you physically in order to feel loved as much as you need to be cherished and desired in order to feel loved. A woman who understands that this area of her marriage is not *just* a physical need for her husband, but is an essential need to his being a man, is treasured beyond measure.

Getting and Keeping His Attention

So how can a wife attract and keep her husband's attention? Men like to chase—after all, they were hunters for thousands of years. To chase and catch a woman is enticing and exciting, and a man wants his woman to be receptive after she is caught. But sometimes if he's disinterested, a wife can try too hard in this area.

If things are not heating up as often as you'd like, try something different, but don't try so hard. If you've been doing everything you can think of short of attacking him, try a new tactic: tone it down a little. Being alluring is sometimes a better way to capture a man's attention than an all-out attack. Some men are intimidated by a sexually aggressive woman. They feel it puts pressure on them to perform, and especially as they get older, pressure is not good. Try letting your husband have the thrill of the chase. Consider wearing something slightly enticing, letting him get a glimpse, then walking away as if you are way too busy to be interested in sex.

Things to Think About

A woman's sexuality may be the most powerful influence she has going for her regarding her man. A woman's strong persuasion in this area can help change, grow, and improve not only her man's life but hers as well.

Unfortunately, a woman who has been sexually abused, especially by her father, often does not recognize this power. Or if she does, she often abuses it. This woman's sexual development has been stunted or cruelly torn asunder by the one man who should have taught her to feel loved and protected by a man. Her innocence was stolen by a thief in the night.

Women who do not enjoy the sexual aspect of their femininity do not fully understand or appreciate the influence they have at their disposal. Some women use their sexuality as a weapon. Some are afraid of the power it gives them and run from it. Some have been damaged so badly in this area that they carry the wounds for a lifetime. For them, their sexuality is a burden, not a blessing.

The healthiest way for a woman to realize the potential of this gift from God is to have her needs for romance met. (See the chapter "Women's Mood #1: Romantic.") She is then able to use her influence in this area in a beneficial and life-giving manner.

Fearfully and Wonderfully Made—Love the fact that God made him so different.

> While women need romance, men don't like or are uncomfortable with romance.
>
> Men look at romance as a prelude to sex and often don't understand a woman's need for nonsexual affection.
>
> When men are physically stimulated, it is difficult for them to focus on anything else.
>
> A man wants to know his woman desires him physically.
>
> Men need variety in this area.

Get inside His Head

> Sex is more than just a physical need for a man.
>
> A man cannot truly feel loved if he is not having his sexual needs satisfied.
>
> Men think about sex often throughout the day.

41

Words Have Meaning

Words That Heal

"I have the best man in the whole world."

"I respect you more than any man I've ever met."

"You are a *good* man."

"I want you—now!"

Words That Hurt

"I have a headache."

"Not again. . . . There must be something wrong with you."

"You just don't turn me on."

"Why can't you be more like [fill in the blank]?"

#2

Work

Every Man's Bane, Every Man's Blessing

Not to be needed is slow death for a man.

John Gray

Work for a man is like talking for a woman. Work seems to be a core part of his essential being. He ties a great deal of his personal value to his work. A friend of mine says that work gives a man the same sense of pride and self-identity as motherhood does a woman. Work satisfies two basic needs in a man—the need to provide for his family and the need to protect his family. Many women think a man's work is just a J-O-B, but it is much more than that. Work allows a man to direct his creative energies into productive outlets. It also fulfills physical, mental, psychological, and emotional needs. Work often defines a man's sense of identity and gives him something he can be proud of. When a man says "I am a physician" or "I am a businessman" or

"I am an ironworker," that expresses part of who he is, not just what he does.

Obviously, tying occupation to self-identity can be an unhealthy thing, and if that's the sole source of a man's self-esteem, it can be disastrous. But notice that one of the first things a man asks another man is what he does for a living. That is an attempt to identify his spot on the masculine food chain and to understand something about the other guy. It immediately tells him a few things about the other man. For instance, if he is a mechanic or a construction worker, he is probably good with his hands; if he is a salesman, he has the gift of gab; if he is a lawyer, he is not to be trusted (just kidding); and if he is a doctor, he's had a lot of schooling and probably makes a healthy income. Also, it often lets one man know the level of respect another man deserves. This can be accurate or misguided, but it serves that function nonetheless.

For instance, a friend of mine has a friend who hangs wallpaper. Upon first hearing, that doesn't seem all that impressive. However, this guy installs huge murals and does complicated restorative work. In truth, he is one of those "if you have to ask, you can't afford me" craftsmen. Wouldn't it be nice if we didn't allocate respect based on job title?

Men also tend to judge or at least filter other men by the amount of income they earn. In that regard, we as a culture tend to hold men who make a lot of money in higher regard than they probably deserve. (Of course, if I made a lot of money I might feel differently.)

Why Men Work

Most men feel compelled to work as part of their makeup. I have worked hard since the age of twelve. But for the past several years I have made a living by writing books and speaking around the country. I also direct our Better Dads ministry. Because I enjoy what I do so much, it does not feel like actual work. Roofing houses, laying asphalt, or hanging Sheetrock— now that's work. What I do is fun. Consequently, sometimes I almost feel that I'm lazy or taking the easy way out. I find myself spending more hours working so that I don't get accused (even by my own self) of slacking off. My wife thinks I spend too much time at my desk, but if I didn't I might feel like I was not fulfilling my role to provide for my family.

It's a bit complicated, but my point is I feel compelled to work even when I really do need to take some time off. I hate to think what a psychologist might say about that attitude. Nevertheless, many men feel that same drive to work.

Because of this compulsion for men to identify and validate themselves through their work (which women generally do not have), wives often misunderstand this drive in their husbands and view it as a negative character trait. Of course, some men do obsess about their work and are distracted at home, not fully engaged in their relationships. This is unhealthy and often is driven by internal wounds or feelings of inadequacy. They feel that if they can be successful and make enough money in their career, then it will somehow prove to themselves and others that they are worthy of respect. In their minds, that will make a woman love them more and lead to a good relationship. That perception is inaccurate and untrue but is how many men unconsciously process the interaction between work and their self-image.

Others consciously or even unconsciously spend more time at work than is healthy for their family. They often do this because work is easier than relationships. Work has boundaries and rules that are clearly defined and tell people when they succeed or fail. It is much easier than the ambiguous and more challenging duties of interacting with a family and having other relationships, which tend to be messier. Men get kudos all the time for their performance at work, but they seldom get a pat on the back for being a good husband, father, or friend. Additionally, if things are rough at home, the workplace can be a haven of peace for many men. They know how to be competent at their job, something they don't always know how to be at home.

Men were meant to work—it's part of their makeup. It is how God made them. Healthy men feel compelled to work—it's almost as if they can't help themselves. In fact, they have a burden to provide that always weighs on their shoulders. Men who work but who are unable to provide adequately are often very frustrated and angered by those circumstances. (Men who couldn't provide for their families during the Great Depression often either killed themselves or ran away to live as hobos rather than face their failure in this area.) They may not always like their jobs, but they know working is one of their key roles in life and so they accept it.

Men who are unable to work at all often suffer from many different kinds of debilitating psychological problems. And men who *choose* not to work often have an unhealthy self-image or self-esteem. Boys raised by the model of a woman being the only provider in their lives often do not develop this strong sense of duty to provide for their families. For males, not knowing about or understanding this key role in their lives leads to frustration and contributes to continuing the cycle of broken families.

Now, men, before you go justifying your long work hours to your wife by telling her that God made you this way and you can't help it, let's look at another perspective. A significant challenge for many men is to recognize that even though God created them with a desire to work, it was actually a curse he delivered on them after the fall. Confronting Adam after he ate from the Tree of Life, God told him that for his entire life he would have to toil painfully and work hard (by the sweat of his brow) in order to survive (Gen. 3:17–19).

Not understanding that concept can give men the illusion that more is better, but in actuality they may just be trying to overcome the curse. And when men forget that and place an overemphasis on work, it could also be that they are being influenced and prompted by negative forces. The evil one, like all great liars, likes to use portions of the truth to deceive us. His goal is to destroy what he hates more than anything else—the image of God as portrayed by a man and woman in marriage. And again, because it is easier for guys to get gratification through achievements and accomplishments than it is through relationships, they tend to overdo it, especially if they are feeling inadequate in those interpersonal areas. Spending too much time at work, or being preoccupied with it when not there, is a trap they fall into that is destructive to them and their relationships.

Now, I actually *like* work and the sense of accomplishment that comes with it. And I've met too many women who hitched their wagon to a deadbeat, lazy guy who won't work to provide for her and her children to give the impression that men shouldn't work hard. But like everything in life, we need the proper perspective. It is human nature to want to overemphasize whatever things meet our needs. So if working makes us feel good about ourselves, we are likely to feel compelled to work all that much more.

Especially with a younger man working to build his career, it is often hard for a wife and family to compete with the emotional stimulus and psychological satisfaction a job or business gives. On the other hand, because it is so tied into his sense of self and value, work can be very stressful when it is not going well. Success at work tells the world he is competent; he is worthy of the mantle of manhood.

Many men have told me that their work is everything. They need to work in order to feel respected, especially by their wives and children. In fact, when I first closed my consulting firm and started full-time ministry, I think I initially detected a certain lack of respect from my teenage son and daughter due to the sudden drop in income. It wasn't obvious disrespect on the surface, but it was definitely there, hidden somewhere deep in their attitudes. And when finances were tough and revenues sagged, I always wondered if I didn't detect just a slight amount of contempt in my wife's attitude as well. It was probably all in my imagination, but it was still a genuine fear.

It could be that even Christians fall into the trap of—subtly or not so subtly—teaching themselves and their kids to judge by economic status. Fortunately for me, Suzanne has now seen enough miracles and lives changed to know God is involved, and it overrides any instinctive lack-of-respect reaction she might have had formerly.

Men have also told me that they understand the burden of not supporting one's wife as a man should. I believe it leads to a wife having a subtle but very real disrespect for her husband, though I also think she'd deny it to her death. It's not a lack of love or abandonment in any sense. It's more like a low-grade fever, which never makes you sick enough to put you down but hampers you nonetheless. I've found that while the love continues, the unease or shaking of confidence a wife feels when her husband is not the hunter-gatherer he should be translates into a low-grade loss of respect that eventually may manifest itself in difficult ways. I don't have a solution for that, but men have to do what they must in order to fulfill their obligations and responsibilities as husbands and fathers.

Perhaps the lesson here is that all of us (men and women) need to learn to be content with what we have and with whatever economic level we are at in life. I don't know too many people, whether they are rich or poor, who don't still yearn for what they don't have. This discontentment in life is destructive and is at the root of many failed relationships.

Of course, every man needs to find a balance between work and family. It's easy for a man to get absorbed in his work because it's easier and safer for him than navigating the many aspects of a relationship. He gets to measure his accomplishments through his work. And young men get caught up in the desire to make their mark in the world. But understand that providing for his family is one of the fundamental drives that God has placed within a healthy man. Men with a healthy masculinity enjoy accomplishing things by meeting goals—it develops their self-esteem. It makes them feel like a man. It makes them feel powerful to be depended on provisionally. To be needed is to be alive.

Men have been called by God to provide. Paul says, "But if anyone does not provide for his own, and especially for those of his household, he has denied the faith and is worse than an unbeliever" (1 Tim. 5:8). Because God created him this way, a man may feel like he is showering his wife with love by working long and hard. A woman can inadvertently sabotage his heart in this area by complaining. For instance, when his wife grouses and complains about how much he works—that she doesn't feel like he loves her because he's gone so much—a man is genuinely confused. The truth is that he is working hard precisely *because* he loves her so much. Often the more dissatisfied his wife is, the more he will work in an attempt to solve the problem, which of course makes the problems of the relationship that much worse. But the man knows no other way than to work all the harder.

Today men as providers are not as important as they were for thousands of years. Their primary role in life has eroded because women are now providers as well. That means that most men do not get the satisfaction and appreciation they crave through working to provide for their families. In the past, men solved problems by working harder. Now when they throw themselves into their work, they compound the problem by being away from their family, creating even more problems. While women file for divorce in this country, they seldom do so because of a lack of financial support. They do so because their emotional needs are not being met. Most men don't realize that until it's too late.

Being appreciated is one of a man's primary needs. He measures himself through his achievements and needs them to be recognized. When a woman seeks appreciation, she is likely seeking to be more understood and validated. Men derive their worth from what they *do*, while women derive their worth from who they *are*.[1]

A Woman's Role

A man's role is to make life easier for his wife and children, not more difficult. One of the major ways he accomplishes this is through providing for them financially and materially.

Many women complain that their husbands have a pre-occupation with work and work-related issues, or that they put work before the family. To keep this in perspective, remember that a man who works hard for his family is better than the alternative. Some women have regretfully been saddled with men who did not feel compelled to support their family. Be that as it may, a woman can use her influence either to make a man's work beneficial to him and the family, or to make it a bone of contention between them. One of her roles is to help her husband balance that fine line between work and family.

Too many men *are* defined by their job, not by the men that God created them to be. But we are all defined not by what we do but by who we are in God's economy. A wife is a powerful influence in creating a healthy self-image in a man. A man works as a gift to himself and an offering to his wife. Providing for her is one way to honor her and tell her he loves her.

Another area a woman needs to remain cognizant about is her husband's career. Many women aren't sure exactly what their husband does for a living. They have some vague idea but really don't understand what he does on a daily basis. A woman in one of our workshops told me she had an image of her husband as the goofy, insecure teenage boy she had first met. But when she went to his office, she was shocked to find out he was actually a high-powered attorney who commanded the respect of hundreds of important people.

My wife has told me how surprised she was when she first visited my engineering firm's office and saw me interacting as an equal with bank presidents, attorneys, city officials, and powerful real-estate developers on a daily basis. It gave her a new perspective on the man her husband was when not in her presence.

Work is a battle and requires a wife's understanding. The paycheck is not the most important thing. A wife must use her intuition and be supportive if the work is affecting her husband's health and their relationship or if a job change is in order. Sometimes a family needs to take on a new standard of living to allow a change in jobs for a better quality of family life. Understand, though, that even if a job is stressful or harmful to a man's health, he will never take a lower-paying position if his wife complains about not having enough money or material goods. Even if a job change would improve his emotional and physical health, he would see it as an affront to his manhood not to support his wife in a manner that satisfies her needs as best as he is able. He will risk his health and longevity to earn his wife's admiration, respect, and contentment in this area. A man will literally work himself to death to give his wife the things she wants.

A woman can greatly influence how much and what kind of work a man does. If you think your husband works too much, take a close look at the messages you might be sending him. Discontentment sends messages of inadequacy, while contentment projects satisfaction. A wise woman recognizes the difference those messages send and encourages her husband to make decisions that benefit him and their relationship in the long term.

Contrast these two scenarios:

Carmen's husband worked long hours. She longed for more time with him. She felt like his focus on work meant that he didn't care about her. Consequently, she started making subtle hints that she would like him to start spending more time at home instead of at work, and while he was home it would be nice if he wasn't always distracted by thinking about work issues. Carmen's husband either didn't hear what she was saying or didn't understand, because he seemed to ignore her requests. As she became more frustrated, she began to vocalize her requests more frequently and with greater volume. She tried everything to get her point across, but her husband just seemed to ignore her repeated requests. Even though she felt bad about coming across as a nag, she didn't know how else to make him understand her need for intimacy. She also felt that his job was unimportant and did not pay enough to meet all their monthly bills. But Carmen's husband would never risk leaving his job or working fewer hours if his wife already felt he was not providing adequately. As Carmen's frustration mounted, they began to argue more often and their relationship steadily deteriorated.

Irene's husband also worked long hours. Irene desired more time with him and suggested that he cut back on his work hours. As expected, Irene's husband didn't seem to process her request; at least, his actions didn't change. Even though frustrated, Irene recognized that nagging or complaining didn't seem to work very well and decided to try a new approach. She started doing two things. First, she gave him frequent positive encouragement regarding his level of provision and how much she appreciated all his hard work. Second, she began to be excited to see him every time he came home from work and let him know how much she loved being with him. After a period of time, Irene's husband began working fewer hours and spending more time at home. As their relationship improved, they started sharing their feelings regarding the work situation. Irene's husband eventually confessed that the more she had complained (nagged) about his job, the less time he *wanted* to spend around her. And when she became more discontented and frustrated, the harder he felt he needed to work to earn enough money to make her happy again.

Two separate women with the same problem—two very different approaches with differing outcomes. Which one was more effective for both spouses?

Fearfully and Wonderfully Made—Love the fact that God made him so different.

Men can't help working.

Men derive satisfaction and self-esteem from work.

When men are working, it is difficult for them to focus on anything else.

Men often work more in order to solve problems in their relationships.

Men need to be needed.

Get inside His Head

A man shows his wife he loves her by working hard to provide for her.

Balance between work and home life is difficult for a man because relationships do not give him the same sense of accomplishment as work does.

Work is important to a man. More than just income, it is part of who he is.

Words Have Meaning

Words That Heal

"Thank you for all the hard work you do to provide for us."

"You are such a good provider."

"I support whatever decision you make regarding your job because I trust you."

"I know your job is important, but Johnny really needs your help to build a car so he can race it in the Pinewood Derby."

Words That Hurt

"You care more about work than you do me."

"Sally's husband always gives her expensive gifts and exotic trips."

"I'm sick of living like this."

"I never have enough money to buy what we need."

3

Play

Win the Game!

A man's maturity: that is to have rediscovered the
seriousness he possessed as a child at play.

Friedrich Nietzsche

Men closely resemble little boys in several ways, but especially in the way they play. I recently spoke at a Dads and Sons camp. For three days we enjoyed skits, songs, and playing together in the beautiful Santa Cruz Mountains. After the first day or so, the shell—that veil of protection that most men have—began to slip off the dads and they started acting more and more like their sons. They rode the zip line across a creek, climbed trees, and endured the ropes course together. The highlight of the camp came on Sunday morning when dads and sons shot off the rockets they'd built together over the weekend. The loudest cheers came for either those rockets that performed magnificently or those that crashed and burned, resulting in near-injury-causing explosions.

As I sat in the back of the room each day before speaking, I watched the dads and sons sing goofy camp songs together and hop around with the dance moves and motions that go along with them. With no women in the room to keep things in check, men and boys both were soon booming out the lyrics and each "bustin' a move" to the beat of the songs—the boys resembling miniature versions of their dads as they were all swept away with the joy of the music. It wasn't the most graceful exhibition I've ever seen, but it certainly was funny!

Boys and men are both drawn to adventure and action, often in the form of play. It's one of the reasons sports are so popular with males of all ages. Because we are made to be performance-oriented, competition is a natural enticement for males.

Competition

Have you ever noticed how competitive men are? My son and I were recently watching the Olympic Games on TV. He came up with a great idea, sort of an Olympics for regular guys—the Man Games. This is where average guys would compete in things men do every day. The events would consist of challenges such as changing tires, mowing lawns, finding and clicking the TV remote (speed channel surfing), making sandwiches, napping, grilling and barbecuing (and its popular sister event—eating brats), and asking directions (where men get dropped off with a car in a strange city and timed on how long it takes them to get back—I anticipate days for some men). Events with a high or dangerous degree of difficulty might be activities like changing diapers, making beds, or loading the dishwasher, using women judges who would score them based on technique, speed, aesthetics, and proficiency. I think men would flock to competitions like these.

Needless to say, competing is part of a man's makeup. Competition plays a big role in a man's life. In fact, a man is always measuring himself against other men. He does so in a number of areas, including (but not limited to) how much income he makes; how physically attractive his wife is; how well his children do in life; how much power he has; his execution of a variety of measurable, performance-based activities; how significant his life is; what kind of "toys" he has; and what he does for a living. This is often not an in-your-face kind of competition but more of an internal measurement.

Some (many) men play like they work—driven, hard, all out, no holds barred. This may make it hard for them to include their wives, who may be looking for a more laid-back kind of recreation. I've known some men who were so competitive at everything they did that their wives and kids didn't want to be any part of it. Men need to control this competitive desire so that their families can enjoy being part of the recreational time.

Men even compete with themselves. I compete against myself all the time. I always try to beat my previous performance no matter what I'm doing. Sometimes that's just getting to the store faster than I did the last time. Every time I write a new book, I hope it's better than the last one. Every time I speak in public, I hope I connect and wow the audience a little better than the time before. And every year, I try to be more successful and make more money than the last. This self-competition drives me to succeed and pushes me to perform even when I would rather sit around on a tropical beach.

Is this competitive mentality healthy for a man? I suspect, like anything, it is and it isn't. Too much of anything is un-

healthy, and competition is no exception. Likewise, too little
of something can also be unhealthy. Men who are too competitive are often obnoxious and destructive in their relationships. Men with no or little competitive drive generally don't
accomplish much in life.

Dreams

Men need dreams. Dreams inspire a man and allow him an escape from the mundane pressures of life. They give him hope.
Sometimes his dreams are just pipe dreams, and sometimes
they are dreams with the potential to become reality.

Even though I am way too old, I still have visions of playing third base for the Dodgers and hitting the game-winning
home run in game seven of the World Series. Picture this: It's
a brilliant, sunshiny Southern California day in October, and
Rick Johnson steps up to the plate with two out in the bottom
of the ninth inning. The Dodgers are down by one run and
on the brink of another year as a team that couldn't clinch
the series. Johnson runs the count full before finally crushing
a towering two-run walk-off home run to dead center field
. . . and the fans go wild.

Or I daydream about rescuing a beautiful woman (my wife,
of course) from terrorists, like James Bond would, using all
my ingenuity, intelligence, and exceptional athleticism. Of
course, this would require me to drive fast cars recklessly
across Europe, jump off high cliffs into blue Caribbean waters, shoot all sorts of large-caliber guns, and demolish at
least twenty bad guys in hand-to-hand combat. Then I would
grab my wife and make a spectacular escape by swinging on
a rope across a deep chasm just before a bomb goes off—all
the while looking dapper in my black tuxedo (although I'd
probably look more like John McClane at the end of a *Die*

Hard movie). And as our lips finally meet, I would stand a bit taller, knowing that I am a hero in my wife's eyes and she is more in love with me than ever.

Or how about an Indiana Jones fantasy?

And don't think I and every other guy in church don't daydream at one time or another about how we would leap up and tackle the nutcase who walks into church with a gun, saving the lives of the women and children in the congregation.

Those kinds of daydreams are fantasy and escapism, which men need to indulge in from time to time.

Like other men, I'm sure, I've also dreamed about helping people, changing their lives, and making a difference in the world. I've yearned to be significant, to make a difference, to have the world know I existed—that I *mattered*. I wasn't sure exactly how I could do that, but because I was willing to take risks to allow God to use me, I now get to see the fulfillment of some of those dreams through the work of our ministry. But it started with a dream that I nurtured in my heart until God was able to fulfill it. My wife encouraged that dream, and that is why I now live the best life I ever dreamed possible.

Playtime

Because men are under a lot of stress and pressure, they need time to relax and blow off steam. A friend of mine stated it this way: "A man needs some playtime—he needs to take out his frustrations on that little white ball. He needs a change from the all-day pressure cooker that his life can be—a time to relax, a time where he can do something of no significance, a time to do something fun."

Because men are physical beings, part of playtime usually includes some form of physical exercise. Little boys play hard on the playground, climbing all over monkey bars, playing kick ball, and wrestling in the dirt. Men often play ball; go bowling, hiking, hunting, or fishing; race cars; or do some other outdoor activity together.

I personally get a lot of exercise—I frequently jump to conclusions. Seriously, though, I like to go to the gym to work out. My idea of a fun day is participating in some good, serious exercise, such as a power-lifting class, and then spending the rest of the day groaning about how sore I am.

You can't pay my wife enough to go to the gym. Her idea of a good day is to read a book and take a nap. As you can imagine, vacationing together presents a challenge. I usually go parasailing while she goes shopping. She's a pretty good sport, though, and most of the time she goes along with me if for no other reason than to make sure I don't seriously injure myself.

Contrary to popular opinion, men like their wives to accompany them in their activities. They like their wives to be their companion while doing things they like to do. It is their way of developing intimacy. Guys that are friends *do* things together. Why wouldn't a man want his wife and companion to do things with him as well?

The word *companion* fits women well. And it is a word that feels good to a man. I like having a companion when I go somewhere or even just watch the ball game. The word *companion* evokes images of a trustworthy, accepting, friendly, and supportive ally. A man needs a companion in life.

One of my favorite things to do with Suzanne is take a walk in the evenings. It is my way of de-stressing from the day. It allows us to talk without distractions such as telephone calls, TV, or radios. Sometimes she doesn't want to go with me, and I am always genuinely disappointed because walking together makes me feel closer to her.

As I write this, she is planning on going wilderness camping with me this summer for the first time ever. I'm excited because she will be sharing one of my favorite activities with me. I'm sure there are other things she'd rather do than carry a fifty-pound backpack a dozen miles into the mountains, sleep on the dirt under the stars, and eat freeze-dried food for days at a time (not to mention having no bathroom). It is something I have been doing for years. She previously told me that at her age, her days of sleeping in the dirt are over and that a five-star hotel is her idea of roughing it. But I think she senses my urgency to share this part of myself with her.

One man told me, "Men *must* have some play in their lives. It helps if their wife is involved. Find common interests and do them often. Do not judge play as childish or immature. Support it, encourage it, participate in it!"

If a woman can understand the need her husband has to balance work with play, she can be a big influence in making sure he is leading a healthier life. In addition, sharing the activities he enjoys builds intimacy and friendship. Men need to play, and they need their women to play with them. Ladies, join your husband—it will make your relationship better.

Fearfully and Wonderfully Made—Love the fact that God made him so different.

Men need to play, especially with other men.

Play for men often involves physical or outdoor activities.

Men need dreams even if they never act on them.

Men don't always like to talk while at play. Talking is not a recreational activity for men.

Most men still have a little boy inside them.

61

Get inside His Head

A man likes his wife to be a companion in things he enjoys doing.

If his wife is dissatisfied with his income, a man will generally not take time off from work to play. If he does, he will not enjoy it.

While work is important, a man gets beat up by it. He needs time off to relax and recharge his battery.

Words Have Meaning

Words That Heal

"I think you should go fishing with the guys for a few days."

"Can I go to the auto show with you? I like to hear you talk about all those hot rods."

"How about taking a couple of days off from work so you and I can get away together alone?"

"I know how much you love bowling, so after work why don't we go to the pro shop so you can get that new bowling ball you want?"

Words That Hurt

"Your stupid dreams will never amount to anything."

"You'd rather play with your friends than spend time with me."

"You're such a little boy sometimes."

"If you spent as much time on chores as you do on your hobbies, we'd live in a really nice home."

#4

Sustenance

Man Does Not Live by Bread Alone

Woman's success in lifting men out of their way of life nearly resembling that of the beasts—who merely hunted and fished for food, who found shelter where they could in jungles, in trees, and caves—was a civilizing triumph.

Mary Ritter Beard, *Woman as Force in History*

Men have certain basic needs (besides sex) that keep them healthy both physically and emotionally. I think a man's needs are less complicated than a woman's, but they are still extremely important from the man's perspective. Getting those basic needs met lays a foundation that men can rely on in order to focus on a healthy relationship. When their needs aren't met, they are more apt to focus on those needs instead of on the relationship. To put it plainly, until a husband's needs are met, he cannot satisfy his wife's needs.

Whether we like it or not, that seems to be true. Perhaps old survival instincts steer a man to focus on himself before being able to focus on others. Again, this may make sense in light of the fact that since the man is the historic sole protector and provider of a clan, his death or illness virtually guaranteed the death of his family. Therefore, it was only logical that a man's needs were met first so that he could then fulfill the needs of others.

Besides sex, men must have these important needs "fed" in order to feel fulfilled and content. They may seem obvious, but they're crucial to a man's well-being.

Food

You'll seldom find men attending an event that doesn't offer food. The concession stands at major sporting events routinely draw more revenue than the paid attendance does. In fact, it's common wisdom that if you want men to come to an event, you have to serve food—the more (and unhealthier) the better. (I can always tell when a woman has influenced the food at a men's event—it includes fruit and low-calorie snacks.) And there is an old adage that our wise old grandmothers recited: the way to a man's heart is through his stomach.

It might be my physiology, but much like a bear, I get pretty grouchy if I go too long between feedings. The truth is I can be downright surly and rude when I'm hungry. My wife has learned over the years that if she wants something, the best time to ask is *after* I've eaten, not before. When my hypoglycemia kicks in, I am less likely to be able to function well. I joke about feeling "faint" from hunger, but that analogy is not far from the truth. I have trouble concentrating on anything other than my stomach when I am hungry. Most men function better if they are fed regularly.

I teach classes in prison, and interestingly, one of the biggest complaints of the men is the quality of the food. You'd think with all the other issues they face on a daily basis (like lack of freedom, potential assaults on their person, etc.) that food would be lower down the list, but time and again I hear how bad the food is.

Being well fed on a consistent basis is a basic need for a man.

Shelter

Men need shelter as protection from the elements but also as a power-based showpiece to tell the world how successful they have been. Additionally, a man will generally try to appease his wife's need and desire for a nice home to nest in. Beyond that, I don't think men put all that much priority on the home.

However, men do enjoy having a clean and pleasant "castle" to come home to in order to relax and escape from the daily stress and pressure they face. A man likes a home that is calm and well ordered. Coming home to the chaos of screaming children and an angry wife is less than soothing to his psyche. Men in ancient times would just go back out hunting if faced with chaos around the cave. Men today often find ways to stay away from that environment—through extra work, hobbies, or even unhealthy activities.

Sleep

A lot of men do not get the sleep they need in order to perform at peak function. I often struggle sleeping at night because the stress and pressures of the day whirl through my mind like a cyclone, picking up speed the closer I come to sleep. Years of pacing the floor at night while my teenage daughter was out on dates have not helped my sleep cycle either.

Many men ignore the need for a proper amount of sleep each night. In the stresses of working and raising a family, it is easy to let sleep slide. Unfortunately, lack of sleep negatively affects many areas of a man's life, including his ability to perform at his job, his physical health, his immune system and ability to regenerate lost functions, his mental health, and even his sexual performance.

As I've gotten older, I've found I need a power nap every so often, usually once an afternoon. A little fifteen- to twenty-minute nap and I am invigorated and ready to go. My agent's wife, Becky, says she studied her husband and noted that if he lacks food or sleep, it affects his mood and ability to get things done. She makes sure he gets something to eat or a nap if he loses focus and has trouble paying attention to details.

A woman can help her husband by observing him and understanding his needs. She needs to get that "PhD" from studying her husband so she can understand what is best for him.

Emotional Support

A man needs a loving wife to take care of him. He needs the emotional nurturing only she can give him. Most men have a shell they present to the world that protects their fragile ego. That ego is fragile not because men are prideful (although some are) but because most of them secretly feel inadequate. Most men generally lower this shell (if just occasionally) only to the one person they trust in the entire world—their wife. It is why a man's wife has the power to destroy him with her words or to empower him to greatness like no one else. Men almost never become vulnerable and trust anyone else by giving them that kind of power over them.

I'm not sure most men consciously recognize this need for emotional nurturing, but in their heart they know they need what a woman brings to the relationship. It is one of the reasons men can be such babies when they are sick—they desire that nurturing touch from a woman. And when the world is beating them up, they need the restorative healing that a woman's touch brings. Her understanding and empathy is important in grounding them when the world crashes down on them.

A woman's belief in a man empowers him like nothing else. His need for her respect and admiration is foundational in his self-esteem and belief in himself. God has empowered women with the ability to nurture men emotionally.

Balance

To be whole and healthy, a man needs to have balance in four major areas of his life. These four areas are connected and overlap one another. Most men do not recognize the connectedness and ignore at least one or more of these areas of their being, and therefore they are top-heavy or tilted in one direction. Being overfocused or underfocused on one or more areas means they are missing out on living a healthy life. For instance, a man who works too much ends up ignoring his family, possibly causing irreparable harm to the relational area of his life. Likewise, a man who spends too much time on hobbies or in school might miss out on several of the other important areas of his life.

The first aspect of this "consciousness" in a man is education. This includes the ability and willingness to be a lifelong learner by attending college or taking classes; reading books;

listening to tapes; or attending workshops, seminars, and retreats. A man needs to continue to learn and be taught by other people in order to stimulate the portion of his personality that thirsts for wisdom and knowledge.

The second part of his entity is spiritual. A man needs to continue to draw into and be discipled toward a closer relationship with God. He needs an adventure in life that gives it significance. He needs to fight a battle between good and evil. He needs a mission. He needs to fulfill his duty to God by discovering and following his path in life. If the spiritual aspect of his being stagnates or is allowed to atrophy from idleness, then he will become myopic in his vision of life. Spirituality requires intentionality. If I am reading the Bible and praying on a daily basis—regardless of whether I "feel" close to God, or regardless of whether I am struggling with a tough situation—my mental, physical, and emotional health is always better.

The third area deals with the relationships of a man's life. This includes a loving relationship with his wife and family. It involves having healthy friendships and mentors in his life. This area seems to be the one a man struggles the most with but may be the most important to his well-being. A good portion of this book is dedicated to helping a man fulfill and satisfy this need in his life.

Lastly, a man needs exercise to ensure that his physical health stays balanced and stimulated. My daughter is much like me in that we are both kinesthetic/tactile learners and very physical beings. We are athletic and stimulated by physical activity. If I do not participate in physical exercise for an extended period of time, say a week or more, my body fails to release certain endorphins and other chemicals that give me a healthy mental and psychological framework. Lack of exercise also causes me to have trouble sleeping, which can contribute to other problems such as depression. Consequently, if I am not exercising regularly, I am often grouchy, stressed-out, and full of anxiety. Because I recognize this, I try to maintain a consistent exercise regime that helps battle the effects of stress and keeps this segment of my being in balance.

Work is also a part of this aspect to a man's character or essence that needs to be balanced, but we talked about that in another chapter, so I have skipped over it here.

Here's how these all work together. Physical exercise helps maintain balance in a man's mental, emotional, and psychological health. Maintaining good relationships also helps with his emotional health, and continuing to learn and educate himself helps with his mental health. Friendships and other relationships stretch and grow his emotional side and keep that portion of his soul fine-tuned.

Most men either do not know or do not recognize this need for balance in their lives. And because men are generally less intuitive and in touch with their beings and bodies than women, they need to understand what makes them tick in order to maintain a healthy presence. A woman can use her intuitive gifts to help her man see when he lacks balance in one or more areas of his life. Her encouragement to participate in activities that develop balance in these areas of his life is crucial to his well-being and, ultimately, their relationship.

Time to Himself

A man needs time to himself. Often when he comes home from work, it takes a while for him to disengage from work mode and transfer into family mode. Time to himself helps him facilitate this change. Additionally, when he has been under a lot of stress and pressure, he may need to get away by himself to feel grounded and get his bearings back.

I frequently speak in front of large crowds. Afterward many people usually want my attention. My wife thrives in that environment. While I function well in that environment for short periods of time, I always need to get away by myself in order to recharge and decompress. If I am forced to continually be "on," I start shutting down. If that continues, I may even become rude toward people (or at least they may perceive my actions that way). My wife knows this and helps me take a short break in our hotel room or some other venue where I can be alone and regroup.

Down Time

> **Vegetate:** 1) to lead a passive existence without using one's body or mind, 2) to engage in relaxing or passive activities, such as watching television, 3) to grow exuberantly or with proliferation

The word *vegetate* has two meanings—it can mean either to germinate and grow or to stagnate. In order to recharge their batteries, men often need to just sit and vegetate. Women frequently recharge themselves by talking with another woman. Just listen to a woman who has been deprived of female companionship for a while when she gets around another woman. She is like a dry sponge soaking up life-giving conversation. She often can't talk fast enough to satisfy her need for conversation.

Because they are wired that way, many women feel they are helping their husbands to de-stress and recover by getting them to talk. Unfortunately, that often has just the opposite effect. Men frequently recharge by cocooning, or pulling into themselves. Conversation is work for most men. Most women do not understand this, but they need to know that it is okay for their husbands to just sit and do nothing occasionally. There may be some logical explanations for this conservation of energy.

Hunter-Gatherer

For thousands of years a man's main role in life was to hunt game to provide food for his family. Because this was a life-or-death situation, every hunt was extremely important—no food meant they literally starved to death. Hence a man needed to be prepared and energized to be able to perform his duty as a hunter whenever an opportunity presented itself. If a man was so tired, run down, injured, sick, or preoccupied that he missed a kill, his family might perish. And the longer or more often he failed, the harder it was to succeed as his strength and stamina diminished. Therefore, whenever a man was not hunting, he was generally conserving his physical and mental energy. Often he sat around staring into a campfire, replaying and learning from previous hunts while resting, preparing, and reenergizing himself for the next hunt.

He also had to be physically prepared to protect his family and the tribe from dangerous predators or human enemies. Any wounds, even minor, needed rest to heal so that he could function effectively. Even a slight injury could put him at a disadvantage (a minor wound in the jungle or woods can quickly get infected and become mortal). If a man were taking a nap because he was exhausted from doing chores around the hut, he and his family could be killed.

Because we do not face constant physical threats in our civilized world, we do not truly understand how important early man was in this protective function. With no police, jails, or criminal justice system, one lone man was the barrier between life and death. His skills and physical strength kept his wife and children alive.

While hunting requires the ability for a man to shut down his mind and stay motionless for long periods of time, it also requires great reserves of energy, especially in sudden bursts of speed and power. For him to stay vigilant for long periods of time using his visual, olfactory, and auditory senses is mentally exhausting. Having the ability to move silently through the woods requires great patience and stamina. Even after striking an animal, he must be able to either move quickly to finish it or spend great amounts of energy tracking it. Finally, he must either field-dress and butcher the carcass or carry it intact all the way back to the camp. Once the adrenaline rush is over, he is depleted. From experience I know that this can be exhausting, and there's nothing more enjoyable than getting back to camp and relaxing while reliving the thrill of the hunt.

Men today, while they seldom are required to hunt in the literal sense, are required to go out and stalk provisions for their family. The emotional and psychological stress of knowing that people depend on them to provide for all their material needs can be a big weight for men to bear. Especially for many men who do not like what they do for a living, it can be terribly draining.

Most men accept this burden with minimal complaining and grousing. But they are challenged mightily every day in a variety of ways in the workplace. There are significant daily challenges to a guy's manhood. These might come from a boss who exerts power over him, from an important customer who is unreasonable but to whom he must kowtow in order to keep his job, or from co-workers who manipulate or use him in order to further their own career. Corporate politics and the wide array of personality types he is forced to deal with can be very challenging.

These trials and confrontations are exhausting to his psyche. The constant barrage of psychological challenges he is required to deal with through cunning and interpersonal communication skills attacks his weaknesses. If he could deal with these challenges in a physical manner, that would be playing into his strengths and would not be quite so debilitating. A man feels beaten down by these types of conflicts and altercations.

Also, the workload and expectations of today's jobs can just plain overload a guy's mental framework. It's like being in the boxing ring with Ray "Boom Boom" Mancini—the punches never stop, and they come at you from every angle.

Lazy or Just Different?

A lot of women I've spoken with over the years harbor a variety of complaints against their husbands. Perhaps one of the most frequent complaints I hear is that they feel their husbands are lazy, that they do not pull their share of the load around the house. They say their husbands are reluctant to perform chores around the house or tackle new projects.

While there may be some validity to these criticisms, I think many of these complaints are unfounded from the standpoint that women look at these issues in a different light than men. For instance, oftentimes when a woman complains that her husband is lazy, it's not so much that he is actually lazy as he just doesn't do things in the order or time frame that she would.

There is a difference between taking some down time and being just plain lazy. If a man is fulfilling his responsibilities as a provider and doing his share of the load around the house, then taking some time off is healthy. If he doesn't have a job and just lies around all day, he's probably lazy. I've seen some women who rag their husbands continuously with "honey-do" projects around the house. They trail around behind their husbands, nipping at their heels to make sure they get the job done right. The poor guys have that slightly hysterical look about them, like horses that have been ridden hard and put away wet.

Recharge

Regardless of the circumstances, men need down time to recharge their batteries. This is not even so much *physical* down time as it is *emotional* and *psychological* down time. They need to regroup and ready themselves for the next day or week's challenges.

One man told me, "There were times when I was a truck driver that I didn't want to do anything at the end of a grueling week. I was tired from three hours of sleep each night and going all day long. I just needed to do nothing so my body could rest and my mind could clear. I think it was mostly a mind issue. It had been busy all day every day, and I just needed some quiet time."

The truth is most men get beat up in a variety of ways through their jobs. Maybe they have a boss that berates them or is unappreciative of their efforts, or perhaps their job is physically straining or emotionally draining. Because I had a child that needed expensive health care coverage, I was forced to work at a job for two years that was under the absolutely worst working conditions imaginable. I worked about ninety-six hours a week. My wife finally made me quit because she could see me dying in front of her eyes. But I did what I had to do, like most men, with an attitude of bleary indifference, if not weary acceptance.

That is why having an opportunity to veg out and recharge his batteries is so important to a man's health and well-being. John Gray, throughout his book *Men Are from Mars, Women Are from Venus*, likens it to "going into his cave" for peace and quiet. Even men who are driven or type A personalities need time to just sit in front of the television occasionally and watch mindless sitcoms or sports programs—modern-day fire gazing. Many men look forward to the weekend as a time to watch a few ball games and reinvigorate themselves for the coming week, when they will be required to expend all their mental, emotional, and psychological energy all over again just to get through the week.

Some men don't like or are disgruntled with their jobs. Oftentimes their jobs are not challenging or stimulating and give no sense of satisfaction. Frequently, they do not feel they are living a life of significance through the work they do. This exacerbates the problem, paralyzing them into inaction and sometimes depression. Even jobs they enjoy can cause stress or frustration.

The opportunity to veg out is necessary to a man's ability to process stress and keep persevering in order to fulfill his obligations in life. It is his modern way of staring into the campfire and preparing himself for the next hunt.

A man needs his wife and the nurturing she brings to the relationship. An attentive spouse can make all the difference in the world to her man's health and happiness. Because a man does not tend to focus on his own best interests (left on his own, he eats junk food and refuses to go to the doctor), he needs a woman in his life to help him stay healthy through her natural nurturing instincts. It's one of the reasons why a man does not do well in life after his wife dies.

He generally gets married right away or else withers away. When he's used to being taken care of, he does not function well on his own.

Wives, you are a blessing to your husband—he just may not realize it. Use your nurturing instincts to help him live as healthy a life as possible. It will benefit you and your husband.

Fearfully and Wonderfully Made—Love the fact that God made him so different.

> Men need proper levels of food, sleep, and emotional nourishment in order to function properly.
>
> A man often cannot focus on others' needs until his sustenance needs are met.
>
> Men often don't fulfill their needs in healthy ways and need a woman's help.
>
> A man frequently needs time to himself. He does not recharge through conversation like many women do.
>
> Men need to balance the different parts of their lives.
>
> Men need down time in order to recharge and de-stress from life's challenges.

Get inside His Head

> *I sure wish my wife would ask me to lie down on the couch and put my head on her lap.*
>
> *I wonder if my wife really appreciates all my hard work.*
>
> Many men do not even know what their nurturing needs are.
>
> Men desire their homes to be tranquil, orderly places in which they can relax and retreat.

Words Have Meaning

Words That Heal

"Honey, you've been working really hard lately. Why don't you just relax and take a nap today."

"How about taking a break? I made you a sandwich and some iced tea."

"You've been under a ton of pressure lately. Why don't you come over here and lie down with your head on my lap for a while?"

"You are so awesome. I just love the way you take care of us."

Words That Hurt

"You only think about yourself!"

"You are so needy."

"I'm not your mother, you know."

"If you want something to eat, go make it yourself."

"Quit being so lazy and help out around here."

"Molly's husband always makes sure the lawn is immaculate."

"How do you ever expect to get anywhere when all you do is sit around watching TV?"

#5

Protector

Guard at the Door

No one can enter the strong man's house and plunder
his property unless he first binds the strong man, and
then he will plunder his house.

Mark 3:27 (NASB)

One of my favorite television shows when I was a kid
was *Have Gun—Will Travel*. Richard Boone played
Paladin (the white knight in chess), a West Point–educated
gentleman-turned-gunfighter. He dressed in fancy duds and
lived a life of refinement until such time as he was contracted
as a champion for hire. He lived in a fancy hotel, ate gourmet
food, drank fine wines, and attended the opera. No mere
assassin, Paladin was a man of morals and conscience who
would try to settle a dispute without violence whenever possible. He would occasionally even turn on his own employers
if he felt they were wrong. When working, he dressed in all

black, used calling cards, wore a holster with the character-
istic chess knight emblem, and carried a derringer. His theme
song referred to him as a "knight without armor in a savage
land." He had a thorough knowledge of ancient history and
classical literature, and he had a passion for legal principles
and the rule of the law.

Paladin was a world traveler who was not just a gunfighter
but also considered himself a protector of the helpless and
disenfranchised. He drew a parallel between his methods and
the movements of the chess piece he was named after: "It's
a chess piece, the most versatile on the board. It can move
in eight different directions, over obstacles, and it's always
unexpected."[1]

Paladin's great advantage over his adversaries was not his
ability as a superior marksman but his rich education. He had
the ability to relate historical events to modern situations.
Like a chess master, he sought control of the board through
superior position, and only killed as a last resort. When the
enemy surrounded him, Paladin could usually make some
insightful comment about General Marcellus and the siege
of Syracuse or something similar, and then use this wisdom
to his advantage. At one point, as he buried a rancher killed
by Indians, he recited John Donne's "Death Be Not Proud."
A male role model who knew poetry was unique on TV in
the 1950s.[2]

Richard Boone made an interesting choice when cast as
Paladin. For most of his career, Boone played the bad guy.
With his scary countenance, gravelly voice, and pockmarked
face with a bulbous nose, he was not your stereotypical hero. I
found the paradox of a homely, smart guy dressed in all black,
portraying a good guy, fascinating. It showed me that you cannot always judge a book by its cover and that appearances are
not always what they seem. But most of all, it taught me that

protecting innocent men, women, and children—especially those who cannot protect themselves—is one of the highest callings of a man. Paladin was not a soft, passive man. He was a "man's man" who used his strength, skills, and talents to right wrongs and protect the innocent.

Guard at the Gate

One of the key innate roles in males is the need to protect what is "his." Even young boys are possessive about things and territories they consider theirs. Of course, protecting what a man or boy considers his can lead to either noble or greedy behavior. In its worst form, this possessive drive turns into selfish, greedy actions. In its best form, passed from father to son, it gives men the courage to lay down their lives for their families. Generally a man teaches a boy the difference between protecting what is his legitimate responsibility and just being greedy. For purposes of this discussion, let's consider "his" to be related to a healthy perspective of his family.

A man protects his wife and children in many ways. He is the guard at the gate of his home. He either allows disreputable characters into his castle or bars their way. These untrustworthy and dishonorable characters approach the gate in the form of friends, movies, television, music, and other forms of influence—some subtle and some not so subtle. Even if a man cannot completely bar these intruders, his impact as a father and husband can counteract these unhealthy influences.

A man's ability to protect his family begins with his involvement in his family members' lives. He spends time with them. They live under the shade of his broad shoulders and feel the security of his protective influence. By spending time with them, his character rubs off on them and his protective influence wraps itself around them. A man must actually have a *relationship* with people so they know he cares about them before he is able to use his influence. Without his physical presence through time spent with his wife and children, his influence is rendered ineffective. Even the strongest man's home is open to invasion if he is never present.

Physical Protection

The most obvious way men guard their families is through physical protection. Criminals and other nefarious types of men who would prey upon women and children generally look for those alone without the protection of an adult male. Just like predators in the wild, they always look for the sick and weak because they are the easiest to kill and the least likely to inflict injury upon them. Men can often sense vulnerability in women and children. Those who have no moral compass use that skill to prey upon those vulnerabilities. It's why single moms and their children are often targeted by bad men. But the presence of a healthy adult male sends those men seeking easier targets.

My presence in the home and with my family when we go places provides a big level of protection for them. My commitment and duty to meet all the young men my daughter dates (even if I don't always want to) decreases the likelihood that she will be with a man that will take advantage of her. In fact, the presence of good men keeps entire neighborhoods from falling into decay and crime.

The truth is that men are so much stronger physically than women, which puts women more at risk than most of them realize. I often see women alone or in pairs walking in dangerous areas or even hiking and camping by themselves in the middle of nowhere. I have to shake my head and wonder what they are thinking. I wonder if television and movies that show a woman defeating dozens of men in hand-to-hand combat have given them a false sense of security and safety.

Even though I have equipped my wife and daughter to protect themselves as best as possible through self-defense courses, pepper spray, and handgun training, I hold no illusions that they would be able to defend themselves against a determined adult male. Their ability to recognize dangerous situations in advance and not to appear vulnerable is probably their best defense. They learn those types of recognition skills from me as a form of protection. By explaining how evil men think, what dangerous situations look like, and how to react in surprising and unexpected circumstances, I have tried to teach them to be best prepared to protect themselves. I have also tried to help them have a long-range vision to recognize situations that could become potentially dangerous—to listen to those premonition feelings in their stomach. That is called protection by prevention.

Of course, there is also safety in numbers. Suzanne regularly hikes in remote areas of the Mount Hood National Forest with a group of her friends. Several years ago I encouraged her to get training and obtain her concealed weapon permit. Since then, several of her friends have followed her lead and each carry handguns while in the wilderness. In addition, most of them bring large dogs along. I pity the fool who thinks this group of middle-aged women are easy prey and tries to bother them, only to find himself in the midst of a gang of irate women drawing down on him with a pack of large dogs snarling by their side. I'd like to see the look on his face—that's a criminal who is going to be in for a big surprise.

Education/Teaching Life Skills

Besides physically, a man protects his wife by having the vision not to put her in circumstances that could be dangerous. For instance, by keeping her car in good working condition, he prevents her from breaking down in a dangerous part of town or on a deserted stretch of highway. My wife likes to run the car down to its last drop of gas before refueling. Every chance I get, I make sure she has gas in her car. I also regularly change the wiper blades, check that the oil and other fluids are filled, and keep the tires properly inflated.

A husband can protect his wife by making sure their budget is within their means and that they don't make risky financial decisions. He might make sure he has adequate life insurance coverage so she and the children are provided for financially should anything happen to him. That way his family is not put in a situation that could potentially compromise their values and safety in order to survive if he were to die unexpectedly. I have met so many women over the years whose husbands died with no life insurance and left them and the children destitute. It seems very irresponsible to me. Women who have been abused or abandoned early in life often tell me they treasure feeling protected above any other mood or need.

A man also helps protect his wife by making sure she is not under the influence of people who would do her harm. That sounds a bit controlling, but I can think of several circumstances over the years in which I felt people who did not have my wife's best interests at heart were influencing her. I had to gently try to point those things out to her so she could make a decision as to whether that was true or not. This can be a very touchy situation and needs to be handled with love and grace and only when you are sure of the circumstances. But I expect my wife to warn me when I might not be aware that people are trying to take advantage of me or deceive me.

In fact, I often rely on her greater intuition abilities and her more developed ability to read people's emotions if I am not sure about their motives. Likewise, as a man, I probably have a greater ability than she does to see through what people say and judge them by their actions and not their words.

As an example, Suzanne and I spoke at a women's retreat recently. One of the other speakers was a man who spoke very eloquently and passionately. He said all the right things and virtually had all of the women in attendance enamored with his holiness and the power of his words. Behind the scenes, though, I began seeing where his actions did not correspond with his words. Instead of being a noble servant of God, he showed signs of being controlling, petty, and self-serving— somewhat of a false prophet. After a period of time it became apparent that he was more of a Fagin-type character from *Oliver Twist*—a father to everyone, controlling them in their brokenness. It took quite a bit of convincing and pointing out examples before my wife was finally able to see his actions above his words.

Men are generally better judges of healthy masculinity than females are. I recently warned a group of single moms about a man similar to the one described above. However, they ignored my advice and continue to seek his counsel. One if them chided me by saying, "We are big girls and can take care of ourselves." Unfortunately, it is obvious, judging by their past choices in life, that they aren't necessarily capable of making healthy decisions (especially about men), and they ignore masculine advice regarding another male at their own peril.

Emotional and Psychological Protection

Another way a man protects his woman is emotionally and psychologically. We'll talk later about a woman's tender heart and easily hurt feelings, how she views the world holistically, and how her nurturing nature causes her to be significantly impacted by hurtful words, actions, and circumstances in her life and in others' lives. One way I protect my wife is by doing the monthly bills and managing our finances. Having formerly owned my own company and now being in full-time ministry has provided many opportunities over the years to experience the mercurial ups and downs that go with financial independence. She stresses out too much when we are struggling financially and would rather not know when we are teetering on the brink of disaster. Some women are blessed with financial skills; she is not.

Another way I have protected her emotional psyche over the years is by not allowing our children to be disrespectful or rude to her. It may be a small thing, but one that many single moms or women with passive husbands are battered by.

And of course I try to help lend her an objective slant during an emotional crisis or confrontation. Sometimes the emotionality of a woman causes her to view circumstances in a more drastic format than necessary or to want to escalate a disagreement unnecessarily. I've observed this many times during the years of having a wife and a teenage daughter in the home.

Watchman on the Wall

God created men to be spiritual leaders and protectors of their wives. Part of the calling or responsibility of men is to be a "watchman on the wall," to stand in the gap spiritually for our families. Men were created to be spiritual warriors or "strongmen." When Mark 3:27 says, "No one can enter the strong man's house and plunder his property unless he first binds the strong man, and then he will plunder his house"

(NASB), it indicates that a man has not only the physical ability but also the spiritual ability to stand in the doorway of his home and block out evil forces. If done properly, not even Satan himself can get past him. This provides a tremendous level of protection and security for his family. Unfortunately, many men are not being spiritual strongmen or are doing it poorly, thus putting their families at risk.

While women have the great ability of "women's intuition," they sometimes appear to be more easily deceived by those who would do them harm. Perhaps their trusting and nurturing nature allows them to more easily believe people are basically good. They also have a propensity to believe people's words above their actions.

A husband can pray for his wife's wisdom and discernment and for her protection from people who would deceive her, to keep her safe in circumstances where he can't. Potential deceivers include well-intentioned gossips, legalistic Pharisees, or misguided religious zealots with distorted biblical doctrine. I have heard some very strange interpretations of biblical theology over the years, even from some well-known, high-profile pastors. Making sure you and your wife stay grounded and in line with healthy biblical principles and guidelines is a powerful form of protection.

A man who wants to be a spiritual leader in his home should read the Word of God (the Bible) aloud to his family (Eph. 5:26). This forms a minimal layer of spiritual protection for them.

God has also given a man the authority to protect his wife or daughter spiritually or otherwise through intercession. In the Old Testament, if a wife or daughter made poor choices or vows, a father or husband had the ability to nullify those decisions (Num. 30:3–8). This was one of the powers of headship God granted men to help them protect those under their charge. This was predicated under the assumption that the head of the family had healthy spiritual discernment and wisdom.

I have even seen men who were new believers have the God-given ability to discern when their wives were getting involved in an unhealthy spiritual environment. One man was able to discern that his wife had gotten involved in a spiritual cult during his absence. Had this man not asserted his authority or had he been complacent in making a decision to remove her from that environment, his wife and family could have suffered significant spiritual consequences.

Another way a man provides spiritual protection is by praying for his wife and daughter. His prayer coverage apparently carries great weight with the Lord (James 5:16). A man can help protect his wife spiritually by praying for her and their marriage, especially if they pray together.

According to pastor and author Will Davis, when a husband and wife pray together daily, their marriage has a 99 percent or greater success rate, compared to the 50 percent national average rate.[3] I know that when Suzanne and I pray together consistently, our relationship is so much closer and more intimate. In fact, entering into fellowship with God together is one of the most intimate activities you can do with another person. That is one reason it is important not to pray with someone else of the opposite sex without the presence of your spouse.

Prayer acts as a shield. It shields those we love from those things that would enslave or destroy them. Can I prove that my prayers have protected my wife and children in situations where they could have been harmed? No, but I believe with all my heart that my (and others') prayer coverage over them did in fact protect them. There are too many situations in life that we as men have no control over, so we must intercede on our family's behalf for the Lord's intervention and protection. If you've ever experienced the helpless feeling of having a child go through a surgical operation, you know what I mean.

Guarding Virtue

When men do not live up to the responsibilities of their most important roles in life—when they abandon or abuse their wives and children, for instance—it sets up generational legacies or cycles that are virtually unstoppable. John Connolly describes perfectly what this looks like in his novel *The Unquiet*:

> Tranquility Pines was filled with screwups, many of whom, curiously, were women: vicious, foul-mouthed harridans who still looked and dressed the same way they did in the eighties, all stone-washed denim and bubble perms, simultaneously hunters and hunted trawling the bars . . . for ratlike men with money to spend, or muscle-bound freaks in wife-beater shirts whose hatred of women gave their temporary partners a respite of sorts from their own self-loathing. Some had kids, and the males among them were well on their way to becoming like the men who shared their mothers' beds, and whom they themselves despised without understanding how close they were to following in their footsteps. The girls, meanwhile, tried to escape their family circumstances by creating families of their own, thereby dooming themselves to become the very women they least desired to emulate.[4]

Again, a man's presence in the life of his wife and children can protect them from these generational cycles that are devastating to a family's lineage. And his example and the model he sets by his presence is capable of breaking previously passed-down cycles. I call this man a "cycle breaker." He's a man who either comes from a broken background and family or enters into a broken family lineage but who turns around and stands firm, doing everything in his power to break that generational cycle. His influence can break hundreds of years of brokenness and wounded spirits. He protects the future of his family.

It's a man's job to guard his wife's virtue. It's a father's job to protect his sons' and daughters' sexual purity, their integrity, and their character. This is not easy and often requires a strong dose of "testicular fortitude." Because his wife is affiliated with him by association, he should be careful that none of his choices compromise her virtue, integrity, or character. In other words, a man's actions reflect on his wife's reputation, just as a wife's actions reflect on her husband's.

Leadership

Maybe more than anything else in life, men feel a duty to protect those under their charge. Men were created to be the leaders and guides of their families. God held Adam responsible for Eve's sin in the Garden of Eden. And today God holds each man responsible for the things he does or doesn't do with regard to leading his wife and children. God gave him authority and headship over his family, which requires him to actually lead his wife and children.

Since God holds men accountable for their leadership, whether they do it or not, how can we best summarize what healthy leadership looks like? There are thousands of books on leadership with about as many definitions for the term. The definition I like best is from speaker David McLaughlin, who says a leader is one who "makes it possible for others to achieve their maximum potential."[5]

Leadership contains two parts in order to function properly: authority and servanthood. Authority is given or delegated by someone in a higher position. God gave a man the authority to lead his wife and family. The best way that a man carries out that directive is by serving his wife. When he doesn't, it leaves a vacuum in the relationship.

Leaders can delegate or even abdicate authority, but they can never delegate responsibility. They are still accountable for their responsibilities, even if they try to hand them off to someone else.

The primary role of leaders is to carry the weight of responsibility. Leaders accept responsibility by making decisions and not blaming others when things go wrong. Some men are reluctant to make decisions because they are afraid of being wrong. But we all make mistakes—no one is perfect. Making a bad or wrong decision is better than not making any decision at all. Since God holds men accountable for their choices—or lack thereof—in leading their families, they may as well take their best shot and make a decision. Men, understand that not making a decision counts just as much as making a decision—sometimes even more.

Frankly, many men feel their wives have unrealistic expectations of them. In fact, most men are confused as to what exactly *is* expected of them. This confusion plays into a woman's complaint that her husband will not lead the family. Truthfully, men are capable of leading their families, but many choose not to. Why? Because of criticism about the way they lead. It's easier just to let their wives do it than to always be second-guessed on their decisions. Rather than risk failure, it is easier just to quit or let someone else do it.

When women understand this important need in a man's character—the need to protect what is his—it explains many of his behaviors and attitudes. He operates in this mode as a fundamental part of his character. It is so strong that men often act on it unconsciously. What may sometimes seem like draconian measures or hard-line decisions might just be a man acting on an unconscious warning that urges him to protect his family. That being said, men need to temper this desire to protect with the need to serve others so that they are able to grow and achieve their full potential in life.

Fearfully and Wonderfully Made—Love the fact that God made him so different.

Being a protector is one of a man's main functions in life.

A man was created to be protective of his family—it is not being controlling.

Men provide not only physical protection but emotional, psychological, and spiritual protection as well.

A man can frequently detect and judge poor character in other men easier than a woman can.

God holds men accountable for the way they lead their families.

Get inside His Head

My wife does not understand how vulnerable she really is.

If I am unable to protect my wife and children adequately, I am less of a man.

It's almost impossible to protect someone who will not let me.

Words Have Meaning

Words That Heal

"Thank you for always looking out for me and the children."

"It makes me feel safe to have you home."

"You are such a big hunk of a man."

"I love the way you lead our family."

Words That Hurt

"You are so controlling sometimes."

"I don't need you to take care of me."

"I'm not helpless, you know."

"If I had to depend on you, we'd all be in trouble."

#6

Connection with God

My Life Matters in the Universe

> I think the purpose of life is to be useful, to be re-
> sponsible, to be honorable, to be compassionate. It is,
> after all, to matter: to count, to stand for something,
> to have made some difference that you lived at all.
>
> Leo Rosen

There's an old joke that says as long as there are math tests, there will always be prayer in school. But the truth is we all have a built-in, innate desire to be close to God. Even when we run from the "hound of heaven" or deny his existence, we know, deep down in our soul, that God exists. (If you have not read the poem "The Hound of Heaven" by Francis Thompson, I encourage you to do so. I am not big on poetry, but this one is awesome, especially if you understand Thompson's background.)

Before becoming a Christian at age forty, I had many encounters with this paradox. I remember being in a near automobile accident once. As time slowed down while the accident was about to happen, my mind automatically, without any conscious thought from me, cried out to God to save me.

When I was younger, a friend of mine and I were driving around after drinking one night. As is likely to happen, we were driving too fast along a winding country road. He lost control, and as we flew over the ditch into the adjacent woods, I could hear him crying over and over, "God, please save me. God, please save me!" When the car stopped rolling and we realized we were not harmed, we started laughing in relief. As we finished laughing and sat trying to control the shakes from the adrenaline surge, I said, "I never knew you believed in God."

"I don't," he said.

"Then why were you yelling for him to save you?"

"I was?"

Here was someone who never acknowledged the existence of God, yet his subconscious knew of the presence of a higher power in the universe when he faced a life-or-death situation.

In June 1981, two months before Suzanne and I were to be married, my little sister Julie, who was scheduled to be a bridesmaid, was killed at the age of seventeen in an automobile accident with a drunk driver. Fifteen years later my stepfather (her biological father) visited and asked if we would go with him to the mausoleum at the cemetery where her ashes were interned. He has never been a religious man and in fact appeared to scorn anyone who believed in God.

As we approached the urn where Julie's ashes lay, my stepfather suddenly broke down and blurted out, "Would someone please pray?" I was so shocked at his unexpected request that I could barely stumble my way through a prayer of condolence. It was so out of character for him that it confirmed even deeper to me the fact that our unconscious knows there is a God despite what our consciousness may say. My stepfather's reflexive need in time of great grief was for the solace and comfort of an almighty, sovereign God, even in the denial of his existence.

If you doubt that intrinsic knowledge of God, offer to pray for someone in deep need. Even the most atheistic individual will accept your prayers and be grateful.

God's Sacrifice

Even after becoming a Christian and studying the gospel of Jesus Christ, I never really understood the sacrifice that God made to have a relationship with us human beings. A thought came into my head one day at church that might come as close as I am capable of to really understanding that concept. I was watching a young father hold his newborn child. The baby was so pure and innocent to my eyes, and the father's love was greatly evident in the way he cooed at and tenderly touched him, kissing his head and marveling over his tiny fingers and features. I then thought, *What if that new father were to willingly give his tiny baby to a group of men who would brutally torture and eventually murder the infant by crucifying him—nailing him to a wooden cross?* Think of the suffering of that tiny baby. Think of the suffering of the father as he watched that brutal scene.

And what if that father had given his baby to those men to sacrifice solely for the benefit of those men, and for other bad or evil people? For people who hated and had contempt for him and his child, or maybe even for people who would never even know, recognize, or appreciate that sacrifice. Or for people who did know about that father's sacrifice but intentionally chose not to accept his magnificent gift—people who were too busy, self-absorbed, misguided, or jaded to care.

That kind of sacrifice might come close to the sacrifice God made so that we could receive his loving grace and forgiveness. Surely I underestimate that sacrifice because my human mind is not capable of understanding the depth and breadth of all the eternal ramifications. But from an emotional standpoint, the above illustration seems most apt to me. This is merely my untrained, layman's way of understanding and coming to terms with that cataclysmic event.

Pastor James Martin of Mount Olivet Church in Portland, Oregon, once said in a sermon, "Jesus did not die for the sake of animals—he died for the sake of people who act like animals." I've come to appreciate that sacrifice because I realized that I am one of those people who act like animals.

A Man's Spirituality

I think men struggle more with developing a deep, spiritual relationship with God than women do. I'm not sure if it's a pride issue, the common do-it-yourself attitude of most men, or just plain apathy. I do know most men don't really seek God until a crisis affects their lives. And many abandon that relationship after the crisis passes. When we are in the midst of battle or the wars of life, we resort to God for help. As the old saying goes, "There are no atheists in foxholes."

Part of this mentality has to do with a man's independent nature. His pride tells him he can or must do things on his own. Part of it probably also has to do with the well-documented feminization of the church in Western culture. Men are consciously and unconsciously uncomfortable worshiping in an environment that looks like the inside of a day spa. And worship songs that tout another man (even if he's omnipotent) as the "lover of my soul" are not very palatable to most men. This is at least a partial explanation for the large number of males (especially minority males) joining the ranks of Islam, which requires sacrifice and performance that men identify with more readily than faith and adulation.

Some men today have discovered that they are more comfortable attending parachurches or home churches. Young men are bored with church, and teenage and college-aged males are leaving in droves.

Frankly, even I struggle with finding a church that satisfies all my needs. I understand that many pastors contend the church's job is to teach the Word of God, but I want a church that is on the edge, that's growing and reaching out to the hurting in the community—a hospital for sinners. I want to be part of something exciting and significant that makes a difference in the world. I don't want to come every Sunday and sit in the same seat, looking at the same people who dress alike and look alike, hearing the same message by the same people over and over again.

It is my opinion that the church is doing a disservice to men, especially young men, by abandoning them. I believe if the church does not change the way it does "business," we will lose a whole generation of young people, eventually becoming a post-Christian nation, as has happened in countries throughout Europe. America may become a nation filled with beautiful but empty cathedrals dotting the landscape. Or perhaps we are already there.

Faith

Faith trumps physical strength, weapons, or manpower. Faith enables us to persevere through powerful obstacles such as despair, trials and tribulations, setbacks, discouragements, and failures. Faith overcomes impossible circumstances and overwhelming odds.

Rare is the man who develops faith apart from the influence of other men. It is seldom an intellectual exercise but is more often nurtured by men he respects. I remember being in many churches before becoming a believer and not seeing any men I respected. Just before accepting Christ, I attended a twenty-year high school reunion in my hometown. I was surprised to find that several of my oldest, best friends had become Christians in the years since I had seen them last. That made a difference in my acceptance and perception of Christians. Shortly thereafter I accepted Christ and was fortunate to start attending a church where there were an abundance of authentically masculine men. I believe that is one of the reasons my conversion "stuck" so well. If I had been around men I did not respect, I probably wouldn't have been too interested in staying.

Part of the problem is the image projected of Christian masculinity. What man wants to be like some of the big-hair guys on TV? Finding other Christian men he can be comfortable with allows him to emulate them and be mentored by them.

One area that we need to be aware of in Christian manhood is behavior-based performance. Many men I know have the attitude, "If *all* God is interested in is how I behave, then I'm not very interested in God." Because men cannot live up to those perfect expectations, many of them either give up or fake it—which might be worse. Unfortunately, those "perfect expectations" often come from other men (church leaders), not from God, who knows we are not capable of meeting that standard. Holy behavior is important and has its place in a man's spirituality, but "behavioral Christianity" lacks depth and is not attractive to most men. We have enough pressure to perform every day without being expected to attain unrealistic goals of holiness.

A man initially gets faith by being vulnerable enough to risk humbling himself before God. Faith then develops through the difficult times and grows experientially. It is a gift from God that can grow based on experience and testimony. I like the saying that faith is spelled R-I-S-K!

God also grows a man's faith through suffering. The same fire that melts wax hardens clay. A true believer who suffers will run *to* God rather than *from* God. What I have found is that as I go through times when I feel overwhelmed and cry out to God, he shows himself to me in new ways I hadn't expected or through his Word, people, or the circumstances I'm in.

As my faith grows, it brings me a surprising gift—wisdom.

Wisdom and Knowledge

When we think about the richest and wisest man in the history of the world, we instantly recollect King Solomon. Most often when we quote from the Bible to explain why Solomon was the richest man, we say that it was because he asked God for wisdom. That's partly true, but he didn't ask God just for wisdom. Solomon asked God for wisdom *and* knowledge. Why would he ask for both of those things? Because one cannot effectively be used without the other.

Many people have knowledge but no wisdom—I know many college graduates (even professors) like that. Young people often have knowledge but lack the wisdom that experience brings along with it. A few people even have wisdom but lack knowledge—for instance, someone from the backwoods with a lot of common sense but no book learning. Both scenarios are ineffective. Those with knowledge of facts and figures but no common sense are doomed to make mistakes and poor choices. Those with wisdom but no education struggle nearly as much because they are unaware of what they don't know. Their wisdom is limited because they have no knowledge in how to share it widely and use it effectively.

A man in either of those circumstances finds himself limited in both his spiritual walk and his ability to live a life of significance. Marriage and parenting require great amounts of wisdom and knowledge to be successful. Having these traits helps a man live a more enjoyable and fulfilled life. The man who stops learning once he leaves school is letting down his wife, his children, and himself.

But even knowledge and wisdom pale in comparison to love. Christian love is not mere emotion or sentiment; it is rooted in knowledge and understanding (Phil. 1:9). As men, we tend to make decisions based on facts and figures as we evaluate people—sort of a performance-based love. The more we learn about them, the more we determine whether they deserve to be given our love or friendship. But as we love our wives *unconditionally*, we gain knowledge and understanding that we cannot get solely by observation or experience. Unconditional love grants understanding and acceptance of our wives, despite the conclusions our observations and experiences might lead toward (Prov. 10:12).

Significance

Many men never read a book after leaving school. Most never continue to grow and learn by attending workshops and seminars. And many never risk attempting challenges that would stretch and grow them. At best, most men work hard to learn a skill to earn a living to support their families. Certainly there is nothing wrong with that in and of itself, as it is one of the main roles God has placed on men's hearts. And they may even continue to learn about their jobs throughout their lifetime, but many never expand that search for knowledge and wisdom to other sources and topics.

This intellectual stagnation limits men in their ability to be significant. To make a difference in the world requires men to take action. But action without knowledge and wisdom is doomed to fail. So even men who do take action often fail, causing them to stay on the sidelines in the future rather than risk being humiliated by failing again.

Perhaps the greatest yearning men have in their hearts and the greatest joy they can experience is to be significant—to matter. John Connolly says it this way:

> It has always seemed to me that there are two types of people in this world: those rendered impotent by the sheer weight of evil it contains . . . who refuse to act because they see no point, and those who choose their battles and fight them to the end, as they understand that to do nothing is infinitely worse than to do something and fail.[1]

Even small actions can make a difference. My experience tells me that most often we don't even know when we are making a difference in someone's life. For example, nearly every month I present classes to inmates at the prisons here in Oregon. The men I speak with are all within six months of getting released and are in a transition program. I almost have to force myself to go to the prison because it is such a spiritually oppressive environment. But God is always faithful to show me the fruits of my labor. Several miraculous events have happened over the years. Recently

I was at the medium-security prison speaking to the men on fathering and authentic masculinity. For many of the men, this is the first time they have ever heard anyone tell them how important they are as fathers and the value their lives have.

Because I am a contractor at this prison, once I enter the facility I am pretty much on my own in the general population. I don't have to be accompanied by a guard like at the maximum-security facilities where I work. This was a little disconcerting at first, as these men are considered to be only a "moderate" risk to health and human safety.

On this day as I was leaving the room after teaching a class, a very large, muscular, bald black man stepped in front of my path, blocking the doorway. Frankly, that didn't seem like a good thing, but because we are taught never to show fear in prison, I continued to walk toward him. As I approached he rumbled, "Mr. Johnson?"

"Yes?"

He held his giant hand out to shake mine and continued, "I can't attend your classes because I don't get out of prison until 2020. But I wanted you to know that every time you come here I sit in that office adjacent to your classroom with the window open and listen to you. I just want you to know how much your coming here has meant to me. It has changed my life. Now I'm trying to reach out to be a father for my children."

I thanked him and tried to swallow the lump in my throat as I headed for the main doors and freedom. If I ever complain about my circumstances, God is quick to show me examples like this that illustrate the significance of the work he is doing through me.

Even though I feel like I fail a lot, I prefer to be one of those people Connolly described who understand that to do nothing is worse than to do something and fail. Men were created to live lives of significance. All men have untapped power within them that is just waiting to be used to change the world. Believe me, if God can use me, he can do truly mighty things through other men. I believe that God is just waiting for a multitude of men in this country to step forward and ask to be used by him. When that happens, stand back. There is going to be an explosion of change like the world has never seen before.

I count myself fortunate to be one of the blessed people who have heard the voice of God. I heard the still, quiet voice of the Holy Spirit in the shower of all places—and it wasn't even a very pleasant conversation. If someone had told me ten or twelve years ago that I would hear the voice of God in my head, I would have thought they were crazy. But I'm getting better at allowing myself to be quiet and listen to God's whisper. I find that I almost cannot listen for it consciously but must try to hear it in the periphery of my conscious mind and auditory range.

Sometimes you can't see something by looking directly at it; you have to look past it to see it. Or other times you can't see something by staring hard at it but can spot it in your peripheral vision. That's how the voice of God is with me. If I concentrate too hard, I can't hear him. I need to invite him in and then relax and let him speak to me on his terms and in his way. It is often more difficult than concentrating and working at it would be.

Men seem to have a different spirituality than women do, or at least they project it differently. Wives, if you want to encourage your husband's spirituality, you can do it more effectively by keeping those differences in mind. Men do not respond well to nagging, complaining, or arguing. Your husband will, however, respond well to your example and the influence of men he respects. God says that your actions speak louder than your words to your husband, according to 1 Peter 3:1–2. (See also 1 Cor. 7:14.) Those verses may apply only to wives of unbelievers, but I think that a wife's actions apply to believing husbands as well. Your faith and the example you set can be a model and an inspiration to your husband. God frequently uses a wife to get to her man's heart.

Fearfully and Wonderfully Made—Love the fact that God made him so different.

Most men struggle with loving a masculine image of God.

Most men do not cry out to God short of a crisis in their lives.

Because men are less relational than women, they struggle with a deep spiritual relationship.

Men are accountable directly to God for the way they lead their family.

Get inside His Head

If my wife understood how boring church is, she wouldn't nag me to go all the time.

Most of the men I meet in church are passive and un-inspiring.

I'm uncomfortable in church, and they do embarrassing things like sing and hold hands.

The guys at work would make fun of me if they knew I was a Christian.

Words Have Meaning

Words That Heal

"I respect you so much for being a spiritual leader in our home."

"What do you think it means in the Bible when it says . . . ?"

"I'm so proud seeing you lead other men and women in the church."

"All the other women in church wish it was their husband doing [fill in the blank] like you do."

Words That Hurt

"Why won't you ever go to church? Don't you know what a poor example you're setting for the kids?"

"You don't go to church because you're just lazy."

"I wish you led devotions in our home like Sally's husband does."

"If you would just pray once in a while, you wouldn't find yourself messing up so much."

7

Guy Time

Friends, Fathers, and Mentors

There is a giant asleep within every man. When that giant awakes, miracles happen.

Frederick Faust

Men need time together with other men. A huge myth has been perpetrated upon the men in this country that we are totally self-sufficient and self-reliant—that we don't need anyone else to get by. This myth has been fueled by a number of segments of our culture, including people who despise masculinity, but at its core it is an attack on the family by evil forces. Men who are alone are much easier targets. They can be picked off in a number of ways: through adulterous affairs, sexual addictions, drug or alcohol abuse, workaholism, fear, or even apathy, passivity, and complacency. Because men are supposed to be the leaders of their families, if they are picked off, their families become vulnerable as well.

Bill was a great father and husband. We knew him and his family for many years and did a lot of things together. Both Bill and I and our families had a lot in common: we were the same age, we both worked from home, we each had a son and daughter the same ages, and we both had beautiful, intelligent wives. As we played together, our families thrived and grew. On the outside Bill had it all—his marriage was solid, his kids were well behaved and happy, and he made a good living. They were like my family in every way.

However, unbeknownst to anyone, Bill was secretly watching pornography on his computer in his home office. This occasional distraction soon turned into an obsession. As Bill fell deeper and deeper into the abyss, he started acting out his fantasies by visiting prostitutes and eventually started snorting cocaine and immersing himself in the dark side of life. Because Bill was an intelligent guy, he was able to cover his tracks so that no one knew what was going on until it was too late. He slowly isolated himself from his friends and family, and even his clients, so that no one knew what was happening. By the time everything came to light, Bill had been forced to close his business, spent all his savings and investments, lost his home to foreclosure, lost his wife and children to divorce, and finally even lost his life to the ravages of HIV/AIDS.

Gradually, over a period of time, Bill's choices fatefully impacted the rest of his family as well. Tragically, without a loving husband to lead her, his wife ended up getting involved with gambling and now lives a life of destitution and bitterness. His children, without the guiding influence of a father, have fared no better. His son grew up angry and made choices similar to those modeled for him by his father. He got involved in drugs and currently resides in the state penitentiary. His daughter, without the healthy masculine affection she needed and craved, started dating men with low character and is currently an unwed teenage mother of two children. She has not gotten a high school degree and has not much hope of living a life of happiness and satisfaction.

Our families were so similar yet went in very different directions. But for the grace of God, my family could just as easily have stumbled off the narrow path of life. It stuns me to know how similar we were and how far we drifted apart. Perhaps only my having other men in my life who provided accountability kept me from suffering the same fate as Bill.

My point is this: a man cannot achieve significance in his life without other men walking beside him. A man needs other men—friends, a father (or father figure), and mentors—to help him face life's great challenges.

Friends

Men need other guys to hang around with and goof off with. It relieves the stress and pressures of life. I am so much more relaxed after hunting or camping with my buddies.

Men also need the accountability friends provide. Our culture portrays successful men as loners, but a man needs friends in his life. A man's friends are his lifeline to a long and successful life. Men who stumble through life alone are more apt to be scared, angry, and miserable.

Men are starving for relationships with other men. Our culture does not create opportunities for men to bond with or relate to other men. The firehouse, however, is an example of a great environment for men. Men in the firehouse work, eat, and sleep with a group of other men for extended periods of time and then get long stretches of time with their families.

111

It seems like an ideal situation for men to bond together and still fulfill their other significant roles in life.

A good friend of mine recently told another man that I was one of the few men he would trust to cover his back in a foxhole. Wow! What an honoring compliment, especially from a man who has persevered through struggles that would have killed an average guy. Who but a friend would tell me something like that? His words made me feel good about who I am. They made me feel like a man. There's just something about a compliment like that coming from another man that makes it all that much more meaningful. My wife tells me she respects and admires me quite often, and that feels good—really good. It motivates me to be a good man—better than I would be otherwise. But there is something fundamentally satisfying about another man respecting, admiring, and liking me for who I am that brings contentment to my soul.

Additionally, for many men there are things they can talk about only to their friends. They cannot talk to their wives about them because women have a hard time understanding certain challenges men face. Only another man is able to relate with and understand them. In fact, it would probably be counterproductive to the relationship if a man were to discuss his true feelings about certain subjects with his wife.

Men need time to let their hair down—a time where they can say and do things that only other guys can appreciate and understand, and a time where they can talk about issues they are dealing with that can only be understood by other men. When women are around, men can never truly relax and be themselves. They always feel pressure to perform or present a false cover. It is part of that gender thing—men are geared to constantly present a "colorful plumage" to the opposite sex as part of the mating dance. Around our friends, that pressure is off and we can truly be ourselves.

Mentors

The most effective way people grow and change is through being mentored. Being mentored by positive role models is also the best way that people, especially males, learn. Males are extremely visual, so the need to actually *see* an example is imperative in their learning and development process.

All males need older males to guide them through life. It is the natural order of things. Even as adults we need other men to help show us the way. We need men in our lives who have been where we're going, who have stumbled where we stumble, who understand the pressures and stresses of being a husband and father and know how to deal with those struggles effectively.

In fact, at every stage of life, all of us need mentors. Boys need older boys. Young fathers need older, experienced fathers to help with questions and problems. Even older males whose children are grown and gone look up to others. I need an older man to show me how to approach the next stage of my life now that my kids are gone.

Oftentimes we don't even realize we're looking for guidance. If we have good role models to follow, then we naturally tend to make good choices in life. With poor role models, however, we tend to make unhealthy or even destructive choices. The advice we get and examples set for us are those we tend to emulate. We learn skills, character traits, and problem-solving abilities from those who guide us.

Because I was not raised by my biological father, one of the joys I experience today is having him available to teach me how to do home repairs and build things. My stepfather didn't teach me those things, and that has been a source of frustration throughout my life. Whenever I needed to repair something, I usually had to try it several times until I taught myself how to do it, not to mention running to the store half a dozen times for the right parts and tools. Having a dad who patiently teaches me how to use my hands to fix or create things is a source of great satisfaction and even comfort to me. Because I have someone to show me how to do things, I am less frustrated and it reduces my anger and anxiety levels.

Boys who do not get proper training from men in their lives never learn how to use the gifts or the power of their masculinity. When that happens, generational cycles such as abuse, addictions, and abandonment get passed from one generation to the next. These young men are preprogrammed to exhibit certain tendencies or make specific choices in life merely by what was modeled for them when they were growing up. They are often not even conscious that they are following in the footsteps laid for them.

Generally, despite our best intentions, our children mimic the worst of the characteristics we model for them instead of the best. They always imitate what we do, not what we say.

I frequently have the opportunity to talk to men in prison, men who swore they would *never* make the same choices that their fathers made, and yet they were almost powerless to keep from falling into the generational sins laid out before them. Because those behaviors are programmed into their subconscious, they come out when least expected.

When fathers abuse or abandon sons, their sons repeat those same behaviors. Even though they desperately might not want to, they almost cannot help imitating what was modeled for them. Only direct intervention in their lives by positive male role models can make a difference. It's one of the powers that God gave to men—we can fix broken boys just by spending time with them.

Men and boys without positive male role models and mentors in their lives often grow up angry and frustrated by the challenges of life. They are often unwilling to accept challenges because of a fear of failure. To fail as a man is humiliating. It's easier to walk away or not even try than to risk the embarrassment of failure.

Fatherless boys frequently grow up to be indecisive, passive, docile, and unable to commit to a relationship. Because they were raised with a feminized vision of life, they tend to rely on females to make all the decisions that govern their lives and seldom take on natural leadership roles. The presence of other adult males in a man's life can help to guide and encourage him to look at the world with a masculine vision and to persevere through struggles until he succeeds, thereby gaining the positive self-image and confidence to accept risk and attempt challenges in other areas of life.

If your husband was raised without strong, positive male role models in his life, he needs to find some good men to hang around with, men who care about him and can teach him things he needs and wants to know. Finding and integrating into a group of men like that can be frightening for a man who is uncomfortable around other men—especially if he has never been accepted into the company of men before.

It might sound illogical, but he may need his wife's help and encouragement to do this. If you as a wife know healthy men, make friends with their wives. This allows a slow, natural process for your husband to get to know their husbands. Eventually, as he hangs around healthy men, he will begin to feel more comfortable and confident. Then your encouragement for him to join in with these men on trips, retreats, and studies will be much more effective. After a while, his confidence will begin to grow and he will start facing life and making decisions as the man he was created to be.

Fathers

No matter how old he is, a man needs a relationship with his father. The curse for so many men is that they never had that relationship. A man needs a father to bless him and help propel him into the world. He needs a father to teach him, model masculine roles for him, and encourage him as he struggles through life. Even a grown man yearns for that kind of approval and blessing from his father.

For any man who had an absent or abusive father, or just a neglectful father, this need will impact his journey through life. It is imperative that a man find a way to reconcile with and forgive his father any grievances (real or imagined) in order to grow and heal from those wounds. If his father has passed on or is not to be found, this can be a difficult journey for a man. But know that these grievances keep him from becoming the kind of man, husband, and father that he is capable of and wants to be. They are roadblocks that prevent his growth as a man in all his roles. They are stumbling blocks that stunt his masculine growth.

I still have not fully reconciled my relationship with my stepfather, but I have been powerfully blessed with a steadily deepening relationship with my biological father, whom I met when I was twenty-four years old. His presence in my life is a blessing of profound magnitude. Having a father who is proud of me and loves me is so encouraging that I can almost feel it bind and heal the wounds accumulated from childhood. His physical closeness is like a cool drink of water on a hot summer day. His unspoken approval fills my soul like a warm, nourishing meal. But most of all, he has given me the ultimate gift—of letting me know I am a man. Without that blessing, I would have, like many men, spent the rest of my life trying to prove to myself and everyone else that I am, in fact, a man.

And yet even with that huge healing gift from my biological father, there is something inside that still yearns for the approval and pride of the man who raised me—my stepfather. I long for him to tell me I am a man and that he approves. Without that I can almost feel a hole in my soul. My stepfather, a broken man himself, is unable or unwilling to grant me that blessing at this time—perhaps because he never received it from his father.

I recently met with a young man who is struggling with a variety of issues, including drug abuse. He had been away for the past year as he bottomed out and then entered drug rehab. He is now trying his best to straighten his life out and become the man he was made to be. As we talked over lunch he made the comment, "I have really missed you."

Even though I'm not his father, I gave him the blessing he yearns to hear from him: "I've missed you too. You are a good man. I have always been proud of you. I believe in you and I believe God has big plans for your life."

Those simple statements brought tears to the eyes of a young man who needs the encouragement and support of a father figure in his life.

Men, if you have a poor relationship or none at all with your father, I want to encourage you to do something about it—for your benefit and for your family's. Approach your father and try to find common ground to start communicating. Consider what kind of man raised your father to see how that might have impacted his life. Tell him you need to talk to him and resolve your issues. Tell him the things you need to know from him. Let him know you forgive him. Start slow but be consistent and patient.

Some of you are thinking that I don't know what I'm asking you to do, that I don't understand how hard that would be. Yes, I do. I have made repeated attempts with my stepfather, but without as much success as I would like.

This will probably be the most difficult endeavor you will ever attempt. It will take more courage than you think possible, because of the potential to be wounded deeply again. I know that I am asking you to risk throwing yourself on the sword again and being hurt once more by the man who has the ability to rip out the core of your manhood. I don't do this lightly. And I'm afraid to tell you that some of you *will* have a sword driven through your hearts again. But the rewards far outweigh the risks. It is the right thing for a man to do, and you need the closure.

In fact, I'd even go so far as to say that if you have the courage to attempt this, it proves you are a man. If you have done all you can and he still does not reciprocate, you have fulfilled your obligation to honor him and can be at peace in your efforts. Worst-case scenario: you are no worse off than you are now with a broken relationship—wounded again, perhaps, but noble in your manhood.

But just imagine if you were able to heal some of those father wounds and have a better relationship with your father as an adult. Wouldn't that be worth the risk? Wouldn't it be worth not passing on some of those wounds to your own children? I think it would.

And ladies, if your husband has unreconciled issues with his father, I want to encourage you to help him. Men struggle with emotions and the intricacies of relationships anyway, but attempting to mend the powerful bond between a father and son is even more formidable, especially when it's been broken and rusted after a long period of disuse. He will need your encouragement to muster the courage to tackle this big challenge. He might be discouraged or even wounded deeply. Attempting this mending takes great reserves of courage on his part and merits your admiration. He will also need your support and healing touch to go through with it. This healing process can take a long time; it's rarely a one-shot deal. Your support will be the difference between success and failure. In fact, he may attempt it only because he realizes it is in the best interests of you and your children. Use all the power that God has given you as a helpmate, nurturer, and completer to stand with him and help him accomplish the journey.

Fearfully and Wonderfully Made—Love the fact that God made him so different.

Men need other men in their lives.

All men need friends, mentors, and a father (or father figure).

Because men are less relational than women, they struggle with finding and developing friendships and other relationships.

Men don't have to talk to enjoy the company of other men.

Men who are not accountable to other men are easy prey for the evil one.

Get inside His Head

If I open up and allow myself to be vulnerable to another man, he won't respect me—or else he'll use it against me.

I'm not going to let myself be hurt by my father again— once was enough.

I'm not going to ask another man to mentor me—he'd probably turn me down or else make fun of me.

I can't mentor another guy—I don't have anything to offer.

Words Have Meaning

Words That Heal

"You should go on that men's retreat—I always get turned on when you return from one."

"Mary's husband would really like to meet you."

"Honey, I am behind you every step of the way if you decide to try reconciling with your father."

"I believe in you."

Words That Hurt

"You don't have any friends; what's wrong with you?"

"Other men that know how to network are more successful."

"You are just like your father."

"If you weren't so pigheaded and stubborn, you could learn something from another man once in a while."

Women's Moods

To be happy with a man you must understand him a
lot and love him a little. To be happy with a woman
you must love her a lot and not try to understand
her at all.

Helen Rowland, *A Guide to Men*

Understanding women and their needs (moods) may
seem at first glance like a monumental task for the average guy. After all, even the father of modern psychoanalysis,
Sigmund Freud, failed to answer the age-old question, "What
do women want?" However, while women are certainly more
complicated than men, there are simple, specific needs they
have that must be met in order for them to thrive. These needs
are even rather logical if viewed with the right perspective!

For instance, despite the protests of radical feminists over
the past forty years, most women do want their husbands to
provide a model of servant-based leadership within the home
and the relationship. I hear this desire expressed frequently

by women of all economic backgrounds and demographics—they desperately want their husbands to be leaders of the home. But this leadership needs to be nurturing and uplifting, not self-serving or oppressive. Even successful, independent career women get tired of always being in control and under the pressure of constantly making decisions. They yearn for a man to provide this kind of leadership in their personal life and relish relying on a man's strong but gentle leadership and provision. In fact, the most frequent complaint I hear from women about their husbands is that they do not lead the family. Due to a variety of factors, many men do not understand what this leadership looks like and how to fulfill this need in a woman's life.

Every man I know wants his wife to be happy and content. It's a mark that a man has done his job well if his wife is content with her life. Plus all men know that an unhappy woman makes everyone around her unhappy. Solomon, perhaps the wisest man in the Bible, talks about a contentious (unhappy, dissatisfied) woman being like the continual dripping of water (Prov. 19:13; 27:15). Even more to the point, "Better to live on a corner of the roof than share a house with a quarrelsome wife" (Prov. 21:9 NIV). I have to believe that Solomon, with all those wives and concubines running around, knew a thing or two about living successfully with women.

I generally do whatever I can to try to make my wife happy. She doesn't ask for much, so this task is usually not that difficult. But she is frequently frustrated when she tries to make me understand what her needs are and I either don't have a clue or miss the clues she's giving me. Generally, this is a case of my not paying attention. One time she wanted me to ask our daughter and her boyfriend to drive with us on a trip. Because I wasn't paying attention to her desires, she repeatedly tried to tell me why it would be a good idea for them to ride along with us. When I finally told the kids to just take their own car, she had had enough and stamped her foot in frustration. It was actually kind of cute, but it definitely got my attention enough to recognize I should meet a need she had. Needless to say, our daughter and her boyfriend rode along with us. Much like Westley in the movie *The Princess Bride*, I often tell my princess bride "as you wish" when she wants something that badly.

The following moods are needs that most women have. If a man can understand these needs, recognize when they should be met in his wife's life, and focus on being a servant leader of his home, it makes life a whole lot easier and more rewarding. Hopefully these chapters will give men some insights and the education they need in order to answer the age-old question, "What do women want?"

Romantic

Romancing the Home

> She walks in beauty, like the night.
>
> Lord Byron

Women love romance. A candlelit dinner, followed by a leisurely walk on the beach while holding hands under the moonlight, is heaven for most women. A luxuriously long bubble bath surrounded with scented candles, followed by a foot massage and a serving of strawberries and chocolate, is just the thing that women crave. Romance is necessary to a woman's emotional health, much like food is to physical health.

Romance is a key factor in having an enjoyable sex life. Women are physically stimulated through romance because it meets their key needs of feeling cherished and loved. Women find sensual attraction and fulfillment through touch, taste, feelings, imagination, lingering conversation, eye contact, and time spent together. Whereas men can be stimulated merely by glimpsing a female body part (or even thinking about one), women need the entire package to arouse their passions. To be romanced is to feel special and valued. It makes a woman feel loved and attractive.

The operative word here is *feel*. Women think emotionally, not logically. And most question their beauty and whether they are truly wanted or not. Nearly all women derive at least some self-esteem or self-value from being desired and wanted by a man. If a man understands her need in this area, he can help her open and bloom like a dew-covered rose in the warm morning sun.

Many women find nonsexual affection such as snuggling, holding hands, or going for walks to be romantic. For other women, just talking with their man is romantic. This kind of interaction develops intimacy with a woman's mate that is essential for her to respond sexually. One woman told me, "Romance means acts of kindness, thoughtfulness, giving me his full attention, and speaking affirming words to me about what I do as a wife, mom, friend, and writer."

Women need an atmosphere where they feel loved without there being an agenda (such as sex). For women, romance may include sex, but it doesn't have to for a situation to be romantic and fulfilling. Another woman said it this way: "I feel less romantic if I feel it is about him getting what he wants and less about him just loving me." Men often look at romance as a means to an end—sex.

But romance is more than just about having or getting sex. Romance serves the purpose of elevating a woman's self-esteem and personal value. When the man in her life exhibits behaviors that make her feel special and wanted by him, she is programmed to respond with affection. Unfortunately, many women get their self-esteem solely from the men in their lives, which gives men too much power to damage their self-esteem. It also puts women (and men) in a no-win situation, as the men are doomed to fail or even abuse this power.

Women and Romance

I find my wife, and most women I've ever met, to be fascinating creatures. Yet they are perplexingly complicated and more often than not very confusing to my more linear, masculine way of thinking.

For instance, my wife generally takes a very convoluted route, meandering down various rabbit trails and exploring an assortment of sidebars, before arriving at the point she wants to make during a conversation. My conversation style is more direct and to the point, without any excess baggage. After all, the shortest route between two points is a straight line. If my wife's conversation style is rambling, then mine is more "as the crow flies."

To some degree, that is how women and men view romance as well. Women like to luxuriate in the sensuous feelings of being pampered, receiving presents, being attended to, hearing sweet nothings, and being touched for long periods of time. A man's view of romance is more linear and straight to the point. Men view romance as a prelude to sex. Romance for a woman serves to make her feel honored, cherished, and loved. One of my wife's friends said:

> As a woman, I need to feel special and appreciated. What would make me feel this way? Give me quality time and conversation that involves active listening. Tell me why I'm special and let me see it in your eyes. Let me feel it in the softness of your touch. A special place to dine, a meaningful gift on special occasions or no occasion at all will reinforce the romance. A smile from across a busy, people-filled room

or a wink . . . just to let me know that you see me and you want me to know I stand out in a crowd, that I'm special to you.

Our daughter is now twenty years old. She recently stopped dating a young man she had been seeing for several years, and young men suddenly came out of the woodwork to ask her out on dates. She found herself being wined and dined at romantic venues every night, and the local flower shop started making regular early morning stops at our house to deliver large bouquets of roses. I explained to her that she is now dating men, not boys. That is how she should expect to be treated by men. A man romances a woman for the pleasure of her company, for the privilege of having her grace and beauty on his arm.

Our daughter is giddy and flush with the excitement of being romanced by a number of eager young men. I, meanwhile, am splitting my time between keeping a steady eye and firm countenance on the young male suitors panting around my daughter and trying to make my wife feel special so that she does not feel neglected in the midst of all the attention her daughter is receiving. Unfortunately, I lack the manic ingenuity and the disposable income of a young man in the throes of pursuit.

Sex

Many women are unable to separate sex from the context of their daily lives and relationships. That might sound strange to us men, but know that if you have been arguing with your wife or if the kids are sick, she is not likely to be in the mood for sex. While men use sex to heal the problems of life, women are just the opposite. In fact, many women report that if the house is messy or the dishes are dirty, they are unable to relax and concentrate on having sexual relations.

Women have a 360-degree view of life—they are much more connected to their environment than men are. Their approach is more holistic. Their physical, mental, and emotional lives are interconnected and tied together. While men can compartmentalize the different areas of their lives (that is, put each subject into a box and not think about it until they want to), women look at the entire picture instead of just its individual components. Unresolved issues, be they relational or environmental, nag at their minds even when they try to forget them. Because of the way they are wired, women cannot just forget about problems for short periods of time like men can, and these problems often make it physically impossible for a woman to enjoy sex.

One woman described her feelings like this:

> If I step back and think about this, I find that more times than not, I fall into "the mood" when things feel "perfect" at home. If things are stressful, unorganized, or chaotic, the last thing I want is to touch or be touched. My surroundings generally put me in the "nesting" mood or the "cycle" mood. But when things are just right . . . I'm romantic. I want to come home, put a little extra lip gloss on, light the candles, make my man his favorite dinner, and go to bed early so we can just be together. I generally feel all mushy inside and most of all content, which seems to fuel my romantic mood.

We men must remember that it takes much more physical contact for our wives to become aroused than it does us. Because their skin is more sensitive, most women find being touched and stroked erotic. A woman I'll call Jessica explained it this way:

I just love it when my husband strokes me when we are just hanging around together. I always tell him he has great hands. A gentle and unhurried rubbing, brushing, stroking brings me goose bumps and immediately relaxes me. (Maybe that's why I love cats. They just come near and rub and purr). This is definitely romance to me. It is not a quick touch but says to me, "I like being next to you. You feel good to me. I like being here and doing this." It isn't the same as sex, but it sure can take me there if he does it when we're lying in bed! I guess sex has more to do with hunger for me. It says he's hungry for me (or I am for him). But stroking says he enjoys me and my company. He wants to hang around and be where he is. He wants to stay a while. Words aren't necessary to tell me he's happy where he is and he's enjoying being with me.

Here's the deal, guys—a man can resolve problems in his relationship by having sex, but a woman can't have sex until the problem is resolved. What a quandary! From my perspective, that means if men want to have sex, they need to be the ones to initiate resolving the problems in the relationship. I hate that part. But since I do like the sex part, I need to step up like a man and initiate talking about the issue in order to resolve it.

Yes, I did say talk about the issue. I don't care for that solution any better than you do, but it seems logical to me that if we want the end result (sex), we need to be willing to take the steps necessary to facilitate that conclusion. And since women process problems by discussing them, we need to talk out our disagreements if we want the benefits. It's similar to getting the sugar cube after taking your medicine.

Also, if a man feeds a woman in the other "mood" areas of this book, romance and sex will naturally follow. When your wife feels beautiful in your eyes, she is more likely to be sexually responsive. That means her husband must be alert for frequent opportunities to compliment her physical appearance so that she feels wanted and treasured.

Additionally, if a man is acting like a man, her responsiveness will be a natural by-product. Being an authentically masculine man means lifting her up and meeting her needs in such a way that she is able to achieve her maximum potential in everything God designed her for and planned for her life.

Meeting Her Needs

For most guys, it's a whole lot easier to be successful in their career than it is in their marriage. But when I stop and think about it, it's often much easier to make my wife happy than I realize. For instance, one thing that really disturbs me is when she calls me at work and starts asking me questions. I know she wants something, and it feels like she's trying to manipulate me. I want to say, "State your business and move on—I'm busy!" Of course if I don't go through the whole "twenty questions" game, she gets hurt feelings and somehow I appear insensitive. But the skills her phone call and questions disrupt (my ability to concentrate, organize, think concisely, attack projects to completion) are the very things that give me the ability to function well at work. And of course she always calls right when I am in the middle of something important or when I am in "the zone" while writing. Nevertheless, I have come to understand that this phone call is her way of connecting with me throughout the day.

For instance, the conversation might go something like this:

"Hello," I say into the phone.

"Hi, honey."

"Hi." Pause. "What do you need?"

"Oh, nothing. I just wanted to see how you were doing."
Pause. "How *are* you doing?"

"I'm fine."

"What are you doing?"

"Well, I'm trying to finish this budget allocation for our
marketing plan for next year. Then I have to get our quarterly
payroll taxes sent out. After that I have an important staff
meeting about the Texas campaign we're designing."

"Oh. So you're busy."

"Yes. Very."

"Oh. Well, you know Joannie? Remember the one with the
little girl who has chicken pox? Well, she told me . . ."

And so it goes as I impatiently listen to a long, involved
story about Joannie and her third cousin's boss's secretary
who was dumped by her boyfriend or some such fascinating
intrigue, so that I can finish and go back to concentrating
on my work.

Especially if your wife is around small children all day,
she needs to connect with you during the day to maintain
her emotional balance and perhaps even her sanity. I have
learned to make an effort to be patient and give Suzanne the
attention and nurturing she needs in order to feel loved and
cherished. It shows her that I care about her.

This need to be cared for as part of the romance package
appears essential to a woman being able to respond to a man
sexually. This type of woman says, "Being cared for fits into
the romantic mood for me. There is nothing like a foot rub
or massage or having a man wash my hair (like in the movie
Out of Africa) to make me feel romantic and cared for. Also,
having a partner who shares the work of supporting a family and home tends to make me feel playful and romantic at
the same time."

Being romantic is often difficult for us men because it is uncomfortable. We run the risk of making fools of ourselves. But understand that the benefits we receive from making our wives feel special and treasured far outweigh the extra effort and risk we take. Often it is not as difficult as we think. Here's how one woman described being romanced:

> I find it romantic when my husband surprises me when he's thought through a special event or gift and I've not had a clue; when he surprises me by making dinner; when he tells me I am smart, wise, or clever. Whenever we do something as a team, I appreciate the moment. It could be cutting down a Christmas tree or talking about our family budget. *If he is fully engaged, then it is romantic.* These moments are rare, and so they are especially sweet. I wish that I knew how to help him be fully engaged. I think I would find it romantic if he would stop me from opening my own door and say, "Let me." Any small expression of care means so much to me.

Women frequently mention the importance of men being "engaged," or being fully aware and not preoccupied while interacting with them, as a part of romance. They feel that when their men are fully engaged and connected with them, they care about them, and consequently it makes the women more interested in sex.

Let me say this as plainly as possible, men. If you want your physical needs met consistently, it behooves you to meet your wife's needs for romance on a consistent basis.

The Chase

Women are wired to feel fulfilled by nonsexual affection. When they receive it, they naturally respond with physical affection. Men are wired to feel fulfilled with sexual affection.

It is a man's responsibility to first serve a woman by honoring and cherishing her with nonsexual affection to ultimately get his physical needs met.

Unfortunately, many men get that turned around. In our desire to get our own needs met, we neglect to fulfill our wives' needs first. A woman has a powerful need to know she is beautiful and sought after. Perhaps the greatest need of every woman is the need to know she is beautiful. To be pursued is to know that.

My wife loves it when I pursue her. A woman should be pursued and fought for as a prize to be won. This makes her feel cherished and makes her more valuable and treasured in the eyes of a man. A man who has had to work hard to "win" a woman's affections appreciates her all the more.

Men enjoy the chase, but unfortunately romance is something that most men are not very good at. The stakes (rejection and humiliation) are too high, and so many men don't even try.

But each woman was created by God with a desire for her husband (Gen. 3:16). Because of that, she has a desire to make herself beautiful in order to attract her husband's attention and affections. She wants to be desired physically by her husband just as she has been wired to desire him. Therefore, it is important for her to hear that she is beautiful.

Guys, your wife needs to hear that you love her, and she needs to hear it frequently. Women tend to place more value on verbal communication than men and so need to hear our love for them.

Oftentimes men feel that our actions (such as working hard) should speak of our love for them, but it's been my experience that women seldom see things like this in the same light. If I get busy doing "important" things like writing, speaking, and running a ministry, Suzanne eventually starts to feel left out. I may be working hard in part to express my love for her by providing. If she feels like she's not getting enough of my attention, she starts to wilt like a flower whose stem has been cut and left out of water. She will even begin acting out a little in order to get my attention. Sometimes that means she will do things just to aggravate me in order to get me to focus attention on her. If I continue to ignore her warning signals, they escalate into serious problems in our relationship.

When I finally get it and start paying proper attention to her needs, she's happy and contented again. Once she's satisfied that I still love her, need her, and desire her, she is fine again for a while. My challenge is to understand that she needs consistent *verbal* expressions of my love for her in the same way I need consistent *physical* expressions of her love for me. If she were to ignore my need for physical attention, I would start getting cranky and act out too.

A woman wants to know that her man thinks about her when she's not in his presence. That's why flowers brought home or sent to her work for no reason are so popular—it tells her you were thinking about her. Obligatory flowers and treats (for anniversaries, birthdays, holidays, doghouse days, etc.), while still necessary, do not earn as many bonus points.

It's been my experience that little things mean a lot to a woman. Cards, little treasures, odd sparkly items, even cheap jewelry seem to mean more to a woman than I can figure out—they're just useless junk to me. I envision even in prehistoric times a caveman bringing home some silly little wilted flower or shiny rock from a hunting trip and being greeted with excitement by his mate. And of course all the other cavewomen would be envious and shoot dirty looks with hands on hips at their men, who are muttering to themselves with their heads down and furtively casting the first caveman looks of resentment and betrayal. Soon all the other cavemen are rather lamely placing wilted flowers at the feet of their own mates to appease their anger and hurt feelings.

Romance is not just a stop along the way to sex. It is an essential part of fulfilling your wife's need to feel loved and desired. She has a compelling need to know she is beautiful in your eyes, and that need requires frequent and consistent reinforcement. Just like men's egos require consistent reinforcement because we secretly feel inadequate, your wife secretly feels undesirable and thus unworthy or even unlovable. Tell her every day that you love her. Then show her you love her by giving her a little romance. You won't be sorry.

Fearfully and Wonderfully Made—Love the fact that God made her so different.

Women enjoy being romanced even if it doesn't end in sex.

Women think with their emotions.

A woman wants to know you are thinking about her in her absence.

Little things like flowers and cards are important to a woman.

Get inside Her Head

Romance is important to a woman because it makes her feel special and cherished.

Romance increases a woman's self-image and self-value.

Romance is fundamental to a woman's happiness and contentment.

Words Have Meaning

Words That Heal

"Honey, you are the most beautiful woman in the world."

"I love you with all my heart."

"You are such a good wife and mother."

"I want to spend the rest of my life with you."

Words That Hurt

"You need to lose weight."

"I don't find you attractive."

"You're only good for one thing."

"Why can't you be more like [fill in the blank]?"

"Bill's wife is hot!"

Nesting

Home Sweet Home

A man would prefer to come home to an unmade
bed and a happy woman than to a neatly made bed
and an angry woman.

Marlene Dietrich

When I married Suzanne in 1981 at the age of twenty-
five, I had been a bachelor since I left home the day
I graduated high school. The apartment I lived in at the time
was pretty spartan: one chair, a television, a bed, and a dresser.
I had one plate (I mostly used paper plates), one glass, and
one set of silverware—oh, and a steak knife. Since I seldom
cooked anything, I had no pots or pans except the broiler
plate that came with the oven. As I remember, the first time
Suzanne looked in my refrigerator, it contained a small jar
of mayonnaise, a few slices of stale cheese, several bottles of
beer, and two eggs. (I'm pretty sure I had at least a box or

two of Kraft macaroni and cheese and a can of chili in the cupboards as well.) I had everything I needed to live contentedly as a single man.

As soon as Suzanne moved in and took over, there was a sudden flurry of purchasing, stocking, shelving, and supplying. It felt as though we were getting outfitted for the end of civilization. Nearly every day we were dragging something heavy up the stairs into the apartment. Since I didn't have much say about the process anyway, I basically just stayed quiet and did what I was told. While she turned my man cave into a home in short order, it all seemed a bit frantic and excessive to me.

A woman has a natural desire to cultivate an environment that best allows her to raise a family. She does this by seeking out an environment with the provision and protection factors in place that allow her to safely have children and then nurture them as they grow. Many women I've spoken with agree with the young mother who said, "It's important to me to feel like my family is well cared for. This includes the house being clean, clothes washed, and meals prepared."

Women care about and value life. They are givers of life. They are born to nurture their children. A woman has a God-ordained role to be a companion to her husband. She completes his life. But she needs to feel safe in order to accomplish these roles. My friend Tim's wife expressed it this way: "I need a feeling of safety. Because we live in a very unsafe world and so much is out of our control, knowing that God is with us is my security . . . but having a man who cares enough to sacrifice day in and day out to provide is very important."

This need for security has been ingrained in a woman's genes from thousands of years of women rearing children and nurturing families. Her natural desire to nurture leads her to feel uncomfortable in unsettled circumstances and more content in a stable, protected environment. A man's natural drive to take risks is often at odds with his wife's nesting instincts. One of the more important aspects that fulfills a woman's need for safety and security and thus allows her to fulfill her role as nurturer is her home or "nest."

Her Home

A woman's home means a lot to her. It is where she raises her children and provides nourishment and sustenance for her family. It is a safe environment to nurture and grow relationships. She desires to make her "nest" comfortable, as it often is a reflection of who she is. Sometimes she's compelled to fluff up or even change her nest around. This is evidenced by the annual ritual of spring cleaning. It is also reflected in those times I come home from a trip to find all the furniture in the house rearranged. It generally takes me about two weeks to keep from stubbing my toe as I navigate around the house in the dark.

One of the challenges my wife and I faced when starting our ministry was the potential of losing our home due to lack of funds. I was surprised at how well Suzanne dealt with that issue, but I also know how much it concerned her. The possibility of losing the home in which she had raised her children and invested so much of herself had to be scary and troubling to her sense of security.

Having a home she can call her own gives a woman a sense of security she cannot get from any other source. A recent seminar attendee expressed the sense of security like this: "My home is my castle. It's my safe place where I can be myself without threat of judgment or rejection. My home is my place to create and express who I am and to bless others through. It's a place to relax and just be me."

Many women will encourage their husbands not to take risks or even job promotions if it threatens their sense of security. Change of any kind is frequently risky and causes concern in most women. To risk losing her home is traumatic and threatens her sense of well-being. Her natural instinct is to avoid or discourage anything that might jeopardize that. She has an aversion to risk taking and typically focuses more on the short-term, immediate needs of her family. This is in contrast to men, who instinctively look to the future and tend to have a long-range outlook on life.

As men and husbands, we need to be aware of this pre-dilection in our wives and base our career decisions around that need for security. My poor wife endured my leaving a secure corporate position to start my own business nearly twenty years ago. I started it right after we had purchased our first home and had two small children. Then three years ago when we (finally) seemed secure again, I launched into full-time ministry, trying to make a living as an author and a speaker. It's a testament to her character and strength that she stuck by me and supported me in each of those situations. Perhaps our strong relationship heightened her sense of security during these changes.

The truth is that security for a woman often comes in forms other than a paycheck. Her relationships are also a big part of having the security she needs to be content and comfortable with her life.

Security

Part of a woman's sense of security is feeling harmony and intimacy in her relationships. The Bible says, "Do not let the sun go down on your wrath" (Eph. 4:26 NKJV). In other words, don't go to bed angry at each other. I wish I were mature enough and a strong enough leader in our relationship to always have followed that advice over the past three decades. Unfortunately, I'm just an average and all-too-human man who fails more than he succeeds. But I have learned that the longer you allow a grievance to grow, the more it intensifies and becomes increasingly difficult to resolve. Unresolved issues create a feeling of discontent and threaten a woman's sense of security. Instead of a man focusing on what *he* needs, he should study her and determine how best to meet her needs.

Women value marriage. It provides extra income, help in raising children, emotional and sexual fulfillment, and someone to partner with and rely on through life's hard times. However, many marriages, especially after children come along, can get dull. That spark of passion goes away. There may still be affection but no real passion. One way to bring passion back for both men and women is through romance. Romance creates anticipation and excitement. Intentionally thinking about ways to excite one's partner and then following through with them often stirs the embers of complacency into a roaring fire of passion. Romance gives a woman a sense of security in her relationship.

Men typically feel compelled to provide materially what *they* think women need. Most men think that women want more cash, a bigger house, money in the bank, and a lot of possessions, because that is how most men determine their own success in life. Some women do want those things; however, a woman's deepest needs are often more relational than monetary. For a man to have a strong, growing, intimate relationship with his wife often makes her feel more secure than a big paycheck coming in does. One of the ways a man can foster that kind of relationship is by being appreciative of her and of all the things she does to make life better.

A husband can encourage his wife by thanking her for providing a good home environment. A friend of mine says that he encourages his wife to spend whatever she wants to fix up two rooms in their home—the kitchen and the bedroom. It makes her feel comfortable, content, and happy to have these two particular rooms how she wants them. She says it's like therapy for her, and since it costs about the same amount of money as going to a psychiatrist, it all evens out in the end.

One couple found themselves in a situation different from the stereotypical norm—he was a neat freak and she was somewhat . . . sloppy. She felt comfortable around clutter. They made a rather unique agreement to resolve this issue. She would minimize her clutter in the rooms he frequented most—the living room and the kitchen. The areas she spent the most time in—her office, the bathroom, and her car—could be as messy as she liked. This worked well for them, as she discovered she could control her clutter in two rooms, but she was overwhelmed to think about having to organize an entire home. As a gesture of appreciation, he frequently cleans up some of her areas. In fact, since their budget allows it, he hired a housekeeper to come in twice a month. It doesn't cost that much to clean the main areas of the house, and it allows his need for cleanliness to be met and her need for some help to be satisfied. I know for a fact that his wife is happier and thankful for his consideration in solving this dilemma.

Men cannot go overboard and expect perfection from their wives, especially in areas that are not their strengths. If you feel the need to have the floor scrubbed twice a week, but your wife doesn't share that need (or she works outside the home too), perhaps you need to bite the bullet and pay for it to be done, or (gasp) do it yourself.

Here's another suggestion for your consideration. Make sure your wife has the tools she needs for the household. Let her buy the things she requires to make her home the way she wants it and to maintain it. I know men who complain about buying a new washer and dryer for their wives yet don't bat an eye about buying a new bass boat for themselves. Dude, trust me, if you meet your wife's needs, she will bend over backward to meet yours. It is truly difficult to out-love and out-give a satisfied woman.

Beyond that, a woman feels pride and a connection with her home that gives her a sense of purpose and even honor. Here's how one woman rather uniquely described the phenomena of nesting and the feelings it evoked in her:

> I remember studying Greek mythology when I was in women's studies in college. I read about Hestia, the Keeper of the Hearth, and it really resonated with me. To be the woman who keeps the home fires burning for her family and spouse appeared to me to be a place of honor and worth in the family unit. To know the woman who creates and keeps a home that is inviting, comfortable, peaceful, and full of joy is to know someone who builds the principles of trust, integrity, and brotherly/familial love, as well as service. For me as a woman and a human being in our society, there seems to be no higher level of need and honor than the woman who is the "Keeper of the Hearth."
>
> I remember writing a paper where I described my delight in housekeeping, as I get a thrill from making my home shine, both literally and figuratively. In fact, when I clean house it is a calming experience, as each object I move brings up the memory of who gave me the object, or who was with me when I bought the object, or what the purpose of the object was in my life. I find it meditative and often insightful as well.

While hers is a unique perspective on housecleaning, it does speak to the powerful need a woman has for a home to call her own.

Home and Hearth

A close friend of ours is approaching middle age and desperately wants two things—to own her own home and to have children. She has a strong need, even craving, for both. Some might say her biological clock is ticking . . . loudly!

For many women, this need for a place to call their own is rooted in their emotional and psychological need for friendship, companionship, and relationships. After all, for thousands of years women raised children as part of a community. They had other women to help them, mentor them, talk with them, and model behaviors such as relating to and loving a man, and being a wife and a mother. This causes women to want to create an environment they can share with others—a place where they can have community.

One woman expressed her feelings about her home by saying, "Making sure my home is comfortable and anyone who enters will feel welcome makes me feel good. I love having people over. I don't feel the need to impress anyone; I just enjoy fellowship."

Another woman felt that her home reflected on her as a person:

> My husband tells me that he really likes when I have get-togethers at our house with family and friends because "our house is always so perfect!" I don't always understand that statement. Don't get me wrong—I keep a clean house, but most days I'm not worried if the lamp shade's seam is facing a direction that could be seen by anyone entering the front living room. But something about having a perfect house for

family and friends to "see" when they come over gives me this little glimmer of being a star! I am the one who is responsible for this perfect home. And even if the praise is directed at us as a whole, I feel good. When everything is in its place, clean and organized, my family feels secure and I feel secure.

This woman may have touched on an important issue—cleanliness of the home is important to the overall well-being of the family. My experience of being a manager at a manufacturing plant and serving in the military has convinced me that a clean and tidy environment promotes good morale, lowers the number of accidents, and gets better performance out of everyone than a sloppy, messy one does.

Whatever the reason, it is important for a husband to understand the value his wife places on having a secure and safe environment to call home. That need gets stronger as she has or prepares to have children. Security is fundamental in her ability to nurture her family. It is a rare woman who is capable of contentedly raising her family in unsettled circumstances (career military wives come to mind). Keeping this need in mind as decisions are made regarding job and logistical choices is instrumental in fulfilling this key mood for a woman. It's a wise man who recognizes this and factors it in to his short- and long-range decision-making process.

Fearfully and Wonderfully Made—Love the fact that God made her so different.

A woman needs a safe and solid place to feel grounded before she can experience security.

A woman's home probably means more to her than it does her husband.

Strong, intimate relationships mean more to a woman than money.

At least some of a woman's self-image is tied into her home.

Part of the reason a woman wants her own home is to fulfill the need for community in her life.

Get inside Her Head

If the house is messy, it is a reflection on me as a woman, wife, and mother.

My home is what keeps our family grounded and together.

If we take any kind of financial risk, we might jeopardize losing the house—that would be an absolute disaster!

Words Have Meaning

Words That Heal

"The mortgage is the most important bill we have to pay every month—I make it a priority to pay on time to make you feel secure and safe."

"The house is yours to do with what you will."

"Sure, you can have as many people over as you want."

"I will never leave you—you are my wife for as long as we live."

Words That Hurt

"Why do you overspend your budget every month?"

"I'm sick of the house being a pigsty all the time."

"You are just like your mother."

"Bob's wife keeps an immaculate house, cooks great meals, and always looks great besides."

Playful

What Are Little Girls Made Of?

Even Nature is observed to have her playful moods
or aspects, of which man sometimes seems to be
the sport.

Henry David Thoreau

Much like all men retain within themselves a part of
a little boy, women also have a little girl deep inside
them that needs to surface occasionally. This portion of a
woman's personality might express itself in playfulness but
might also feel vulnerable, feel fragile, and have a need to lean
on her husband. In this mood she doesn't need romance but
instead might need to pour out her thoughts, be listened to,
or derive some soothing comfort from her husband. Similarly,
at times a little boy might be hurt and worried and need
nurturing, and other times he might just want to play down
the street with the other boys.

149

Let's look at some of the facets of this mood that indicate your wife may have needs to be met.

Flirtatious and Playful

One way a woman expresses herself in this mood is to get girlish and playful. (But if a woman's need for security has not been met, she will have a hard time enjoying this playful facet of her personality.) In this mood she may want to act like a little girl and play in the flowers—so let her. She might be flirtatious, play music, sing, dance, or spin in a circle so that her dress twirls around her. In this mood my wife gets slightly giddy, but she needs to trust that I will not call her silly or needy. One woman said, "Tickle me, pursue me, hold me while we talk. Reassure me that you are my best friend, my protector and provider. Let me know that I am your special someone. Spoil me, entertain me, fix something for me that is broken. Let me be weaker than you. Tease me tenderly, sensitively. Let me expose the little girl hidden within, and be my hero."

My wife likes to flirt with me when we are in the middle of a business or ministry meeting. In fact, it seems the more formal and reserved the occasion, the more she likes to flirt. I find it a bit distracting and even awkward but try not to let my annoyance show. I'm trying to focus on an objective while she is trying to connect and develop intimacy with me, which puts us at a crossroads with each other.

Men tend to think more analytically than women, who, as we've discussed, often process information more holistically, if not emotionally as well. My focusing on her, even in the midst of serious discussions, means to her that I love her. It satisfies any insecurities or nervousness she may be feeling at the time. She likes to be reassured that I find her beautiful, captivating, attractive, and desirable. She wants to know if I really believe that, and if so, that I will act as if I do. Then she will respond with confidence and be generous with her love and in her actions toward me. She won't feel as if she needs to be guarded, that her "mushy" love directed at me goes unappreciated and unwanted. She knows I am busy but wants me to find a moment here and there to just appreciate her.

She also likes to play sometimes. This frivolous time might include my tickling or chasing her or our lying together in a meadow looking up at the sky. Perhaps just my good-natured teasing tells her I love and respect her. Again, it means my focus is on her and I am not distracted by other matters. She loves spending time together playing board games, talking, going on a picnic, or just sitting together listening to music. Other times she might want to hike, play golf, go boating or bowling, or even play softball. What seems to be most important to her is that I remember to include her in my life and not be preoccupied with other things too frequently when I am with her.

Dreams

Most women have a creative side to them that needs to be expressed. A woman needs her own "garden" of creativity to tend, a place she can go to be refreshed and invigorated. This plot will get bigger as the children grow older, when many women feel free to start actively tending their dreams that they have been holding on to while raising the kids. Oftentimes women who spend all day raising children don't feel like they are using their gifts and talents to contribute to the world.

This creative side can be expressed in as many different ways as there are different women. For some it is working in the garden, for others arranging flowers. They may paint or sculpt. Some have hobbies such as scrapbooking, quilting, knitting, book or card clubs, dancing, or playing an instrument. Others can soak in nature in the outdoors, either through a quiet walk in the woods or through physical activities such as kayaking, biking, horseback riding, or rock climbing. They may quietly curl up and read a good book or just have some time to themselves to dream and decompress from the pressures of life. For some women, going back to work, going back to school, or changing careers may be a way to stimulate their creative energy.

Because women are such creative beings (they create and nurture life), the ability to make things gives them a sense of peace and satisfaction. Learning a new task or accomplishing something is rewarding and stimulating. Because they constantly use their multitasking skills, this creative side allows them a release to express themselves.

Find ways to help your wife create and tend her literal or figurative garden. With small children, a woman may be able to tend this side of her personality only in small doses. Give her time to clear her head and do something just for herself. Let her have a personal day during the week to spend by herself where she can go to a bookstore or the library, go to the gym, or walk the aisles of the local farmer's market. Ask yourself, *My wife put her dreams on hold for me and the kids. What can I do to help her tend her dreams?*

Because we men are typically more task oriented, we often don't understand this creative side of women. While we're creative too (we rebuild cars, do woodwork, or collect things), our creativity is often goal oriented or performance based, whereas a woman's tends to be more nurturing and revitalizing.

Her dreams are important to her, and they need to be tended. If you can do this for her, you will have a much more satisfied and contented woman on your hands. That spells good news for you no matter how you slice the cake.

Goals

Because of the sacrificial nature of nurturing and raising children, many women set aside their goals and plans until after the children have grown. It's a huge sacrifice to make in the bigger picture of things. To set aside twenty years of your life in a cause to raise and nurture children and a family is a sacrifice I'm not sure most men would be willing to endure. Striving for my dreams and the goals I've set in life is something I've been accustomed to for most of my life. Certainly I have forfeited a few things along the way, but for the most part my life has been about me while still within the context of fulfilling my responsibilities and obligations.

Yet many women make that sacrifice gladly. Once the kids are older or grown and gone, it is a good time for them to revisit their goals. This might mean going back to college and getting a degree, or beginning or going back to a career they started years before.

Many women are also now starting their own businesses. *Working Mother* magazine reported that women-owned businesses open at twice the rate of male-owned businesses. According to the US Census Bureau, women-owned businesses employed nearly 9.2 million workers as of 2002. The US Small Business Administration reports that women-owned businesses generated $2.38 trillion annually in revenues for the US economy.[1]

We know one woman who, after the children went off to college, started her own scrapbooking company that has grown from a simple home business to a rather large international company. She combined a hobby she enjoyed with her goal to create a business and is now reaping the benefits. She found that many of the skills she employed as a stay-at-home mother for all those years—like organizational and interpersonal communication skills—helped her as a businesswoman.

Fragile

The other side of this playful aspect to a woman's personality is that sometimes she becomes fragile and needs a lift to get her back into the groove. Because women are created with more hormones and are more complex physiologically, it often means that their highs are higher and their lows are lower than men's. In these situations, a man can be a big support by understanding what she is feeling and helping her feel better about her world.

One way to know when my wife is feeling vulnerable is to note how she describes it when she is in this mood. She feels overwhelmed and paralyzed, her head gets fuzzy, and she can't do even little tasks. When this happens, she needs me to just hold her and listen to everything she says. Sometimes I have to give her a differing perspective on life. For instance, when she is discouraged I might need to show her how she is positively touching the lives of those around her. I need to give her some encouragement and help her to look at a "treetop" view of her life—the big picture. When she is fragile, she might need me to make her some soup or give her a foot massage. I also need to encourage her during these low-mood days to have a cry, take a nice long bubble bath, get into some snuggly pajamas, and watch a cooking show on TV. Not exactly how I would tend to myself, but it is what she needs to heal and pamper herself.

A woman is a complex, multilayered creature who needs to be stimulated in a variety of areas in order to be fulfilled. She has a creative side that needs to be tended and nurtured. She needs to be able to feel safe and protected by her husband when she is feeling vulnerable or scared. This allows her to feel secure enough to be playful when she needs to relax. The ability to play with someone means she has an authentic intimacy with that person.

Lastly, she has likely set aside or sacrificed her life goals for the benefit of her family. When she decides to achieve those goals, she will need your support and encouragement. That's what masculine leadership does—it helps people achieve their potential and lifts them up to be all they want and desire.

Fearfully and Wonderfully Made—Love the fact that God made her so different.

> Women have a little girl side that needs to express itself through playfulness.
>
> Women need to be encouraged to nurture their creative side.
>
> When they have a family, many women set aside their goals and dreams to focus on nurturing their children.
>
> Women are complex creatures who need to express their many facets in order to feel fulfilled.

Get inside Her Head

> *I love it when my husband playfully chases me and isn't so serious.*
>
> *What good is life if you can't have fun once in a while?*
>
> *I wonder if I could ever become a sculptor?*

155

I've always wanted to go back to school but don't know if I should or not.

Words Have Meaning

Words That Heal

"Sure, I'll rototill the side yard so you can plant a garden."

"Let's go to the park and play on the merry-go-round."

"If you want to start a business, I think it's a great idea. What can I do to be supportive?"

"Honey, now that the kids are grown, what have you always wanted to do with your life?"

Words That Hurt

"Quit acting silly all the time."

"I can't deal with your Peter Pan attitude anymore."

"Grow up and take responsibility for your life."

"Dreams are just that. They are never meant to be real."

Nurturing

Tending the Nest

If a woman has to choose between catching a fly ball and saving an infant's life, she will choose to save the infant's life without even considering if there are men on base.

Dave Barry

I f men were created for the roles of providing and protecting, then one of the most significant roles God gave to women is that of nurturing.

God designed your wife to be more nurturing than you. Without her gifts in this area, a family would never be able to survive, much less thrive. (Admit it, guys—left up to you, the kids would eat way more pizza and burgers than is healthy, and you'd all wear the same clothes several times over before they hit the washing machine.)

A wife has the capability of being empathetic whenever anyone is feeling bad, comforting when they are wounded, and healing when they are in pain. She is more often than not caring, kind, thoughtful, gentle, compassionate, loving, and sensitive. She feels compelled to make sure the children are safe, fed properly, washed, and clean with all their needs met. Her presence helps children thrive and grow like vigorous stalks of corn in fertile soil. Her nurturing instincts bring vitality to family life. Her healing touch cures everything from scraped knees to bruised egos. Her gentle compassion soothes even the most horrendous betrayal.

Women love to encourage and support other people in their search for meaning in their lives. They love to share their life experiences with one another. They like to help others with their problems.

Women are the nurturers of the family that keep it functioning and growing. Frankly, the mortality rate would probably be a lot higher if men were left alone to their own devices with their children. Quite a few of us guys have forgotten our toddlers somewhere and had to go back and get them, or have inadvertently let something happen to them that narrowly avoided a disaster—which fortunately our wives never found out about.

But because women have bigger hearts than men do, they are also more easily broken. I think Peter referred to a woman as the "weaker" vessel not as an insult to her mental or physiological strength, but for her more fragile and tender heart (1 Peter 3:7).

Tender Mercies

Our wives are a lot more tenderhearted than we are. Women are more gentle and caring about people and their feelings.

Women tend to be more unconditional in their love, while men are more performance-based in theirs. Women are generally more accepting of others and their faults than men are. Women are more apt to fall for a sob story or try to rescue someone who claims to have been mistreated. They are more attuned to their emotions and sensitive to nuances and shifts in relationships. In fact, their thinking process is fueled by emotion, hence they think emotionally rather than in a linear fashion like men do. Men think of things in a logical progression—in other words, if we do this and then that, this will be the result (A + B = C)—but women's minds think of many different, and often unrelated, topics all at the same time. Men compartmentalize their thoughts and emotions, but women think on many levels. And the billions of synapses between the neurons of a typical woman's brain all appear to connect with each other in a frenzy of information overload (at least from the perspective of a linear-thinking being).

Have you ever been talking to your wife and suddenly realize you have no idea what she's talking about because it is a completely different subject than you were just discussing? I often wonder how the two (or three, or six) different subjects my wife is talking about could possibly be interrelated. When she explains the process that connects them, I am often astounded at the complexity involved. (She once talked her way out of a traffic ticket by confusing the male police officer so much about what a frozen turkey had to do with her speeding that he finally just walked away and let her go with a warning.) The mere mention of someone's name can send her thought process off in a direction completely different from the topic at hand. Judging from my wife's explanation of her thought process and her conversations, I would be frightened inside her head. It would be like being trapped in a carnival fun house while suffering from a bad case of hallucinatory malaria.

I was a speaker at a Mothers of Preschoolers (MOPS) convention one year and almost died because I found myself trapped in a room where five thousand women were all talking at the same time about every unrelated topic under the sun. My mental circuitry was overloading and frying as I tried to process all that illogical data input.

Words Count

Sometimes it's hard for us men to understand and realize how fragile a woman's psyche is, and we can easily or inadvertently crush her spirit with our words or actions. Sometimes I have to think, *I've seen her pop out a baby and hardly break a sweat, so why in the heck is she crying over a couple of words I said?* I've learned over the years that she often takes my words more seriously than I mean them.

Remember that while men get validation from achievements, women get it through their relationships. Words mean a great deal to women, and women have a need to hear words that validate their worth. They need to hear that they are loved and needed. In fact, you'll notice that women use a lot of words—two to three times as many as men.

Women crave compliments. If you want to see the heart of even the angriest woman melt, just tell her how beautiful she is or say something like, "Baby, you know how much I love you." Even if she suspects you are lying, she will still *want* to believe you.

Your wife needs to hear several things daily. She needs confirmation that you love her, and she needs to know you find her attractive physically. I think if a man were smart enough to tell his wife those two things every day, she would be a pretty satisfied woman. She needs to hear those things frequently to allay her fears and insecurities.

Your wife, like most women, is very insecure about her appearance. She magnifies in her mind any perceived imperfections or flaws in her physical appearance. I use the word *perceived* because they are usually just that—figments of her imagination. The great mystery is that even the world's most beautiful women think they are ugly or have features they are insecure about. So your wife greatly needs and desires to hear from you, "You're beautiful" or "You are gorgeous." Occasionally she likes to know she looks sexy as well, but not all the time (also, women don't seem to like being called "hot" for some reason—perhaps because they think it's a cheaper version of sexy).

In this area, your words are very powerful. Remember that verbal communication or words mean a lot to a woman—more than your actions do most of the time. Her craving to know she is appealing and beautiful makes her subject to even insincere flattery. She wants to know she is needed and wanted by you.

Notice how men who have learned to speak a woman's language are very successful with sexual conquests. They learn to tell women what they crave to hear: that they are beautiful, desirable, and irresistible. Of course, they don't actually mean it, but many women fall under their spell anyway.

Nurturing the Nurturer

Even the way your wife is wired biologically contributes to this nurturing ability she has. Recent studies at the University of Pennsylvania performed MRI brain scans on men and women. The experimenters induced stress in the subjects by having them count backwards as quickly as possible from

1,600 by 13. Imaging showed that while under stress, more blood flow went to the prefrontal cortex in men, the area of the brain that induces a fight-or-flight response. In women, more blood flow went to the limbic system of the brain, the area responsible for "tend and befriend," or nurturing, behavior.[1]

This explanation might be one reason why women seem to be better able to juggle the massive and often stressful roles of raising small children on a daily basis. I think most men would fold under the burden of raising small children and taking care of a household full-time. Sure, there are some men who are stay-at-home dads, but they are the exception, not the rule.

So how can a husband help his wife best use her gifts of nurturing? One way is to meet her needs. Here's how one woman described her needs in this area:

> When I am upset or hurting in the midst of difficult situations, please stand by me and be the support I need, a best friend. I need your strength to get through these times; your listening ear, your soothing, caring voice to let me know it's going to be okay. Can I depend on you to be there? Will you pray so my strength in the Lord can be built up when I'm unable to pray for myself or my situation?

One of the very few complaints I have had about my wife during the course of our long marriage is that she doesn't keep as clean a house as I would like. It's not that she's dirty or keeps an unclean home; it's just not as orderly as I would like it. Having a spotless home is not as high on her priority list as it is on mine—she would rather have fun and enjoy life.

This was something that bugged me for years. I finally realized a couple of things. First, if I wanted the house kept to my standards, I was going to have to do the majority of the housework. (Note—I discovered that housework was not my favorite activity.) And second, it could be worse. There are a lot worse things she could do than neglect a little housework—she could have sexual hang-ups and be absent in the bedroom; she could be unfaithful; she could be rude, disrespectful, or contemptuous toward me; she could be a lousy cook or any number of other things that would make my life miserable. I realized that by helping instead of harping in an area that she was probably never going to change in anyway, it helped to nurture those sides of her that benefited me and others in our family.

Another way a husband can help his wife is by giving her breaks so she can reenergize and nurture herself. Guys, you all know how difficult it is, even for short periods, to watch a couple of little curtain climbers bouncing off the walls. Yes, you can make it look easy in the short term because you can play with them for a couple of hours, but secretly most of you are glad when your wife gets home and can "take over" the job of watching them.

Now imagine having to be around them every second of the day, 24 hours a day, 7 days a week, 365 days a year— providing for all their needs, not having a minute alone, always on guard. Never being able to watch the game on TV for a few minutes for fear the two-year-old would be toddling down the freeway, or the four-year-old would be flushing the remote control down the toilet after shaving her head with an electric razor, or the five-year-old would put snakes and bugs in his little sister's bed even as he "paints" her face with Desitin. How about changing *all* (or most anyway) of the poopy diapers, even in the middle of the night, even when you're sick!

That could frustrate and even depress the strongest person. The pressure of constantly being with young children can be debilitating after a period of time, and frankly, I'm not sure how women do it. That doesn't even count all the household chores, cooking, cleaning, and scheduling, on top of meeting all *your* needs as well (and if you're being honest, guys, you know how many needs you have).

Especially when women have young children, they are so harried by being "Mom" to everyone and everything that they sometimes feel like they lose their identity. They feel like they are nothing but servants and caretakers of everyone around them. The constant neediness of everyone overwhelms their sense of being. This is also the time when a woman's history— any dysfunctional issues from childhood—can surface and she won't even know why.

Men, here's a simple suggestion that I want to encourage you to consider. Since your happiness and your family's depends directly on your wife's nurturing abilities, it only makes sense to help her stay as healthy as possible in this area. In order for her to stay healthy and recharge herself, I suggest you give her at least a one-hour break every day.

Now some of you might be inwardly groaning as you read that, but let me put it in perspective. If your boss made one hour of overtime mandatory every day, you probably wouldn't complain too much, you'd just suck it up and get it done. So if you were to take an extra fifteen minutes when you pull into the driveway to decompress from your workday, then go in the house, change clothes, and offer to watch the kids for an hour, it could make an amazing transformation in your marriage. Your wife could leave and do whatever she needed to do, allowing her to gather her sanity, talk with other adults, and catch her breath. It wouldn't be that difficult if you just considered it a little bit of overtime for each workday, and I promise it would make a world of difference to your wife. If she knew she could count on this time every day, she would start looking forward to it and be happy to see you walk in the door. Your wife would be happier and healthier, and her nurturing instincts would be even more honed and inspired. When that happens, you will be the one who benefits most.

The truth is, guys, we need women to help us be civilized, focused, ambitious, connected, healthy, and happy. Women are our anchors and connection to love, family, and meaning in life.[2] That means it is our responsibility to seek our wives' best interests, even at our own expense.[3]

There's another old saying that relates to the practice of making sure your wife is taken care of. Old sayings always make a lot of sense when you figure out how they apply to your life. This one says, "Ain't no one happy if Momma ain't happy." If you make sure your wife is happy, you can be sure that you will be happy as well.

Fearfully and Wonderfully Made—Love the fact that God made her so different.

Women usually believe a person's words over their actions.

Generally speaking, women are more compassionate, loving, and understanding than men.

Women tend to be more tenderhearted than men and consequently have their feelings hurt more easily.

Your wife needs to have daily confirmation that you love her.

Without women, men's lives would be very hard and unemotional indeed.

Get inside Her Head

That poor little stray puppy needs some food and loving. The kids need vegetables for dinner, not ice cream.

I feel so bad when my son is picked on at school—I've got to go rescue him!

If we can just figure out what is going on with the Johnsons, we can help improve their marriage.

He needs a good woman to take care of him. I have a friend who would be perfect for him. Maybe I can fix them up on a date.

Words Have Meaning

Words That Heal

"I love the fact that you take such good care of me and the kids."

"The boys and I couldn't survive without you."

"Sure, you can keep that stray cat."

"Thank you for all you bring to our home."

Words That Hurt

"You are so weak—you believe every sob story someone gives you."

"Would you please quit mothering me!"

"You are so needy."

"Quit acting like a baby—you get your feelings hurt too easily."

Cycle

The Moon and the Tide

Every month, it is woman's fate to face the abyss of
time and being, the abyss which is herself.

Camille Paglia

All women are subject to a hormonal cycle each month
(or every twenty-eight days on average). For most men,
this process is mysterious and more than a little scary. Most
of us feel this subject is strictly on a need-to-know basis
and we don't want too much information. But I think it is
important for us to have more than just superficial knowledge to understand what changes our wives go through each
month. Understanding this cycle may help explain many of
the behaviors of women that are confusing to most men. So
here is a quick primer on a woman's menstrual cycle.

Menstrual Cycle

During menstruation (a period), a woman's body sheds the lining of the uterus (womb). Menstrual blood flows from the uterus through the cervix and out of the body through the vagina. Most menstrual periods last from three to seven days.

Menstruation is part of the menstrual cycle, which prepares a woman's body for pregnancy each month. Hormones rise and fall (sometimes dramatically) during the month to make the menstrual cycle happen.

According to the US Department of Health and Human Services, in the first half of the cycle, levels of estrogen (the female hormone) start to rise and make the lining of the uterus grow and thicken. At the same time, an egg in one of the ovaries starts to mature. About halfway through a typical twenty-eight-day cycle, the egg leaves the ovary in a process called ovulation.

The egg then travels through the fallopian tube to the uterus. Hormone levels rise and prepare the uterine lining for pregnancy. A woman is most likely to become pregnant the three days before ovulation or on the day of ovulation. If the egg is fertilized by a man's sperm cell and attaches to the uterine wall, the woman becomes pregnant. If the egg is not fertilized, it will break apart, after which hormone levels drop and the thickened uterine lining is shed.[1]

During the menstrual cycle, many women experience symptoms associated with premenstrual syndrome (PMS), a normal part of the cycle. Typically PMS is characterized by anxiety, irritability, and mood swings. Most likely, these symptoms are related to the balance between estrogen and progesterone produced in the body. If there's more estrogen, anxiety occurs. If there's more progesterone, depression may be a bigger factor.

Cramping is one of the most common discomforts women have during menstruation. There are two kinds of cramping, spasmodic and congestive. Spasmodic cramping is probably caused by chemicals that affect muscle tension. Some of these chemicals cause relaxation and some cause constriction. Congestive cramping causes the body to retain fluids and salt.

Fatigue, headaches, and sugar cravings are also related to PMS. Women may crave chocolate, white bread, white rice, pastries, and noodles as well. (Judging from these symptoms, I'm guessing I might frequently suffer from PMS.) These food cravings may be due to higher hormone levels before menstruation, which cause increased responsiveness to insulin, at which point women may experience symptoms of low blood sugar. In these circumstances, a consistent diet that includes complex carbohydrates can provide a steady flow of energy to the brain and counter the ups and downs of blood sugar variations.[2]

Other symptoms of PMS include acne, bloating, weight gain, tender or swollen breasts, cramping, constipation, nausea, and mood swings. During pregnancy and for some time after childbirth, menstruation is normally suspended, although not always. (However, pregnancy carries with it its own series of delightful complications, including swollen and tender breasts, fatigue, tiredness, nausea and morning sickness, backaches, headaches, frequent urination, stretch marks, and food cravings.)

There are also several complications that can make menstruation very painful for women or girls. Premenstrual water retention frequently accompanies menstruation for many women. Water retention makes a woman feel bloated—it causes her breasts to become uncomfortably enlarged, her feet or ankles to swell, and her stomach to feel thick.

According to the website Medline Plus, while some pain (cramps) during menstruation is normal, excessive pain is not.

> The medical term for excessively painful periods is dysmenorrhea. There are two general types of dysmenorrhea. Primary dysmenorrhea refers to menstrual pain that occurs in otherwise healthy women. This type of pain is not related to any specific problems with the uterus or other pelvic organs. Secondary dysmenorrhea is menstrual pain that is attributed to some underlying disease or structural abnormality, either within or outside the uterus.[3]

The hormone prostaglandin, produced in the uterus, is thought to be a factor in primary dysmenorrhea. This hormone causes the uterus to contract, and levels tend to be much higher in women with severe menstrual pain than in women who experience mild or no menstrual pain.[4]

With all that complicated activity going on, I'm pretty glad I'm a man. About all I have to do is make sure I'm fed and maintain my body and I'm generally okay. Because of all those complex goings-on in a woman's body, significant side effects can manifest themselves during her cycle.

Hormone Mania

The hormone fluctuations a woman experiences frequently cause her to act easily hurt, angry, irritable, unreasonable, or illogical at times. I don't know if this cycle contributes to or promotes disharmony in the home, but I have my suspicions. I haven't done any scientific studies to confirm my theory, but after having had a wife and a teenage daughter in the home together, I do know there were specific times each month when things seemed pretty chaotic and frazzled around the home front. Much like coming face-to-face with a grizzly bear in the wilderness, there have been times where I had to follow the "do not make eye contact—back away slowly" strategy to escape physical harm. Real or perceived slights and hurts were magnified, and expectations seemed (at least to me and my son) unrealistic. The women in our home were irritable, easily hurt and offended, defensive, and even downright angry during this time. They acted illogically and irrationally and even appeared to suffer from temporary insanity. It's no mystery to me why ancient tribes used to segregate women from the clan during this time of the month.

Having grown up with two sisters and then having a wife and daughter in my home, I've seen my share of irrational and illogical behavior over the years—much of it unexplainable even by the women themselves. Just recently I made the mistake of mentioning that a particular blouse my wife had bought was less than flattering on her—it made her look heavier than she actually was. You'd think that after twenty-seven years, I'd be smart enough to know better. However, I thought I was doing her a favor mentioning this just before we went out to dinner because she had previously gotten mad at me for *not* mentioning that an article of clothing didn't look good on her. She had just lost a lot of weight and looked really good. I didn't think she would want to wear something unflattering. But after reattaching my head from having it bitten off, I was pretty confused about what I'm supposed to say and what I'm not supposed to say (not to mention when).

Many women I speak with tell me funny stories about their friends' behavior during this time of the month. This kind of irrational behavior seems pretty consistent in most women. One woman said:

171

Emotional Phases of a Woman's Cycle

First Week (after her period)

- Estrogen levels rising
- Self-directed, disciplined
- Outgoing
- Task oriented and focused
- Reasonable
- Optimistic

Second Week

- Estrogen levels off and declines slightly
- Blue skies—summer-like feelings, happy, hopeful, easygoing
- Sense of well-being, inner strength
- Less assertive, more realistic goals than first week
- Peaceful, not bothered by small irritations, enjoys loveliness of environment
- Creative with positive energy
- Feels reasonable and tolerant of self and others

Ovulation (approximately ten days following end of period)

- Estrogen rising again, progesterone rising
- Passive, introverted, or patiently accepting and open-minded
- Content and nurturing feelings
- Especially amorous and interested in lovemaking
- Might have odd cravings (as in pregnancy)

Third Week

- Rising estrogen and sharp rise in progesterone
- Subject to variable feelings—some good, some bad, up and down
- Moody and gloomy—sense of feeling doomed, apprehensive without reason
- Slowing down—disliking pressure
- Feeling immobilized, doubting herself
- Discouraged, less friendly and outgoing
- Losing sense of well-being, longing for more peaceful life
- Impatient with others, losing interest in goals and plans, bored
- Lacking coordination and clarity of thought (PMS "fog")

Fourth Week: Premenstrual (estrogen and progesterone levels fall)

- Very reactive, irritable, touchy, nervous, unable to concentrate
- Moody, unstable, quarrelsome, unpredictable outbursts of emotions
- Sensitive to noise, food binges, craves sweets or spices
- Childlike, unreasonable
- Lack of self-confidence, loss of interest in hobbies and tasks
- Melancholy, withdrawn, awkward, shaky[5]

Hormones do strange things to our bodies and minds. We feel ugly and fat, and our self-image and self-esteem are affected, sometimes dramatically. We don't know why we feel sad or irritable. Our feelings are on our shoulders, ready to be hurt at any given moment or opportunity. There may or may not be a reason. Our emotions are all over the board. Logic does not have a place. So please just listen and empathize as best you can. Don't try to fix it.

Our friends Ron and Terri tell the story of the time they were driving down the road on the way to church. They had not been married long and Ron was still learning the ways of Terri's moods and cycles. For no reason at all Terri suddenly began crying. Ron asked her, "Why are you crying?"

"I don't know," she sobbed.

Nonplussed, Ron asked, "Well, what should I do?"

"I don't know. . . . Ask God."

After several minutes of solemn prayer, Ron looked at her in all seriousness and said, "He doesn't know either."

Terri burst into laughter and the storm soon passed.

Unexpected Behavior

A recent study conducted on the neurochemistry of the brain during menstruation shows there may be some significant biological causes for a woman's erratic behavior during menses.

Using a technique called functional magnetic resonance imaging (fMRI), the scientists looked at blood oxygen patterns in women's brains at two stages of their monthly cycle, just before menstruation and around a week after. The scans showed that all of the women in the experiment had more electrical activity in the frontal lobe of the brain during the premenstrual phase, the time when most women might experience PMS.

Most often when PMS was present, the scientists saw dramatic differences between the scans. They found that when a woman feels good, "her deep limbic system is calm and cool and she has good activity in her temporal lobes and prefrontal cortex. Right before her period, when she feels the worst, her deep limbic system is often overactive and she has poor activity in her temporal lobes and prefrontal cortex."[6]

According to studies performed by Dr. Daniel G. Amen, PMS symptoms are detectable in brain scans. His studies show that two distinct PMS patterns occur that respond to different treatments. One pattern involved increased deep limbic activity, often accompanied by excessive activity in the temporal lobe. This activity correlates with cyclic mood changes.

> When the limbic system is more active on the left side, it is often associated with anger, irritability, and expressed negative emotion. When it is more active on the right side, it is often associated with sadness, emotional withdrawal, anxiety, and repressed negative emotion. Left-sided abnormalities are more a problem for other people (outwardly directed anger and irritability), while right-sided overactivity is more an internal problem.[7]

The second PMS pattern noted was increased deep limbic activity and increased activity in the cingulate gyrus, which is the area of the brain associated with shifting attention. Women with this pattern often complain of sadness, worry, and negative thoughts and verbalizations.[8]

What Helps

There are several natural options and activities that reportedly help relieve the discomfort associated with menstruation. These suggestions were gathered from a variety of sources cited earlier in the chapter, as well as from a number of women's comments from an email survey. They are not meant to be medical advice but merely suggestions to help with discomfort. Any serious or ongoing problems should be discussed with your physician. Guys, by being aware of these remedies you can help make sure your wife takes care of herself properly and suffers less as a result.

Diet

As noted earlier, one of the main discomforts associated with a woman's period is congestive cramping, which causes the body to retain fluids and salt. To counter congestive cramping, it is recommended that a woman avoid wheat and dairy products, alcohol, caffeine, and refined sugar. Caffeine constricts blood vessels and increases tension. While menstruating, refrain from drinking caffeinated drinks such as coffee, tea, cola, or cocoa.

Reportedly, eating smaller, more frequent meals that are high in complex carbohydrates, along with taking a daily multivitamin with calcium, is helpful as well. Eat lots of fresh vegetables, whole grains, nuts, seeds, and fruit. Avoid red meat, refined sugars, milk, and fatty foods. Putting cayenne pepper on food was also suggested. It is a vasodilator (it widens the lumen of blood vessels) and improves circulation.

Anecdotal information also suggests that eliminating NutraSweet from the diet will significantly relieve menstrual cramps. If you drink sugar-free sodas or other forms of Nutra-Sweet, try eliminating them completely for two months and see what happens.

Take a multivitamin every day that includes four hundred micrograms of folic acid. A calcium supplement with vitamin

D can help keep bones strong and may help ease some PMS symptoms.

De-stress

Avoiding stress and finding ways to relax apparently help alleviate many symptoms associated with PMS. Meditating and deep-breathing exercises help to eliminate strain and pressure. Find healthy ways to cope with stress—talk to your friends, exercise, or write in a journal.

Also, a massage works wonders. You may find that keeping your abdomen warm with a hot water bottle or something similar works as well.

Lastly, take time for yourself. Pampering yourself and taking care of your needs keeps stress at bay and improves your mental and emotional outlook.

Other Options to Alleviate Cramping

Exercise regularly. This will improve blood and oxygen circulation throughout the body, including the pelvis. Get enough sleep. Try to get eight hours of sleep each night. Don't smoke. Try not to use tampons. Many women find that

---

What Can a Husband Do to Help?

Offer her a foot massage or a back rub. Head massages are nice as well.

Offer to cook dinner and then do the dishes afterward.

Bring her a hot water bag and encourage her to take a nap.

Give her a day off from chores by doing them yourself without even letting her know.

Take the kids to the store, or watch the kids and allow her to go shopping by herself.

Light some candles around the tub and draw her a nice hot bath.

Give her free time alone to meditate, journal, or talk with friends.

---

tampons increase cramping. Don't use an IUD (intrauterine device) as your birth control method.

Finally, over-the-counter pain relievers such as ibuprofen, aspirin, or naproxen may help ease cramps, headaches, backaches, and breast tenderness.

If you're like me, guys, I'm glad I'm a man and less complex physiologically than a woman. Frankly, not having to deal with all these complicated issues every month for the majority of my life is just fine with me. However, learning about what women go through makes me more understanding and empathetic.

Much like the myths perpetrated upon masculinity, such as sex being just a "physical" need or men having fragile egos because they are prideful, there are legitimate reasons why women appear irrational and behave strangely during their menstruation period. However, the stereotype of women using this time of the month as an excuse for poor behavior has been exacerbated by those women who abuse the presence of their symptoms to justify their attitudes, or by unscrupulous defense attorneys trying to make a name for themselves in high-profile trials.

In several recent criminal trials, the defense attorney used the "PMS Defense." This is where the defendant tries (sometimes successfully) to use the symptoms of PMS as a defense or a mitigating factor to excuse criminal behavior including drunk driving, assault, and even murder. That seems to be tantamount to a man using "midlife crisis" as an excuse to dump his wife for a younger woman. Those women who genuinely suffer from exaggerated symptoms (and, in fact, all women) have paid the price for this malfeasance of the truth by people who should know better.

Understanding your wife's struggles during this "mood" of her life will help you to meet her needs and be less frustrated by the side effects. And not to put too selfish of a spin on this, but once a woman's needs are met, it's hard to out-give her, and you'll benefit because of your efforts.

Fearfully and Wonderfully Made—Love the fact that God made her so different.

All women have a monthly cycle that includes menstruation (a period).

Part of this cycle includes experiencing unpleasant side effects.

Hormones released in the body can cause a woman to act irrationally at least periodically.

A woman needs her husband's understanding and support from time to time in this area.

Get inside Her Head

I don't know why, but I feel like I want to rip someone's head off.

I am crabby and bloated.

I feel like staying in bed and crying all day.

These cramps hurt so bad, but if I complain he'll think I'm using them as an excuse.

Chocolate—I need chocolate!

Words Have Meaning

Words That Heal

"How would you like a foot rub, sweetheart?"

178

"I'll take the kids. Why don't you go take a nap while I get dinner ready?"

"Can I get you anything from the store?"

"How about a nice, warm bath before bedtime?"

Words That Hurt

"Would you stop complaining all the time? It can't be that bad."

"You must be a hypochondriac."

"You're just using this as an excuse because you don't want to go."

"I don't see other women acting like you do."

Spiritual

"My Sweet Baby Girl"

> When it comes to little girls, God the father has nothing on father, the god. It's an awesome responsibility.
>
> Frank Pittman, in *Women and Their Fathers*

We have a great big gray-and-white tuxedo cat named George that lives with us. George weighs between twenty and twenty-five pounds depending on how many times he's eaten that day (which is a pretty constant occurrence). Even though he's hefty, he's also a beast—heavily muscled and slightly belligerent. He's so powerful that if we put a harness on him, he could probably pull a cart if he had to. I've always been a dog kind of guy, but I really like George. In fact, he's more like a dog than a cat—he comes when you call his name, and he likes to be patted solidly on

181

his haunches and back. He only likes men; for some reason he can't stand women, which irritates my wife and daughter to no end.

Unlike most cats, George generally does not like being stroked or sitting on anyone's lap. He will occasionally jump up on my lap in the recliner, but he weighs so much that my legs soon fall asleep and I find myself irritating him until he gets exasperated and jumps off. Lastly, he's lazy. All he does is eat, poop, and sleep. George's one and only hobby in life is terrorizing Riley, our cowardly one-hundred-pound Lab/shepherd mix. As you know, "stuff" runs downhill, so whenever George gets messed with, Riley ends up catching the brunt of it.

Despite all that, I find I like George's disdainful character. My son or I will often scoop him up, flop him over a shoulder like a half-full bag of flour, and squeeze him until he gets exasperated and squeaks in protest (George cannot meow for some reason). But either he really likes it or he's too dumb to know any better, because even though he fights to get away, he generally comes right back repeatedly for more torture.

The other day I scooped him up and squeezed the stuffing out of him, and after I let him go, he huffed several times and stared at me reproachfully. I told him not to get mad because I could pick him up again if I wanted to—in fact, I could do anything I wanted to him. (Yes, I apparently do spend too much time in the office by myself, evidenced by the fact that I talk to a cat.)

Then it struck me: *I wonder if that's how God feels about me sometimes.* He just enjoys picking me up and squeezing me until I squawk, and somehow he derives joy from doing something occasionally that aggravates me. I know that's probably not true, and of course it flies in the face of most serious theological perceptions of God, but I can't help wondering sometimes if God doesn't mess with me just because he can. It sure seems that way. I believe God has a great sense of humor, and I wouldn't put it past him to play a prank on me every now and then. Some of the methods he uses to teach me lessons sure seem to have a humorous side about them, anyway.

But that might be more of a man's perception of God than a woman's. Women, I think, tend to have a larger, deeper, and perhaps more personal relationship with God than do most men. They are more willing to submit to his omniscience and humble themselves before him. They probably hold him in greater awe than men do (or at least are willing to admit through their actions). It has been my observation that women tend to pray and worship more deeply than men do. Look around in church during worship service—it is most often the women with their hands raised, their eyes closed, and tears streaming down their faces. They are able to let themselves go more easily in communion with the Holy Spirit. In fact, because they are more relational and intuitive, they may be able to access the Holy Spirit more easily than men.

Because women are more relational, I think they tend to have a deeper relationship with God. They are probably more able to love or be *in* love with the masculine image of a heavenly Father than most men are. While I fear God greatly (which is the beginning of wisdom) and I feel like I have a close relationship with him, I generally do not feel like he is my "lover," my husband, the lover of my soul, my soul mate, or any of the other terms of endearment that worship songs attribute to him. That probably closes off a certain intimacy in our relationship that a woman might be able to access more readily.

I'm always a little suspect of the man who claims to be "in love" with Jesus. Men like this are rare. They are the exception, not the rule. When you do see these men, they are noticeably different and stand out from the average guy. Truthfully, I'm not even sure I know exactly what it means for a man to love Jesus with all his heart. Perhaps that's a flaw on my part, but I don't know that I have been through enough struggles or suffered enough to truly love and appreciate God.

I also hear people tell me how much their children "love Jesus with all their heart." Perhaps so, but it seems to me that to love someone requires them to grow together through experiences, some good and some bad. You tend to become closer to someone, or love them more deeply, when you have gone through difficult or trying times, such as war or other life-and-death circumstances together. Maybe I'm wrong here and God's love and grace transcend growth and maturity. But it has been my observation that many men don't "love" Jesus. To love someone would imply that you would take action for their benefit. I'm not sure I see that action evidenced by many men in the church.

I tell women all the time to judge men by their actions, not their words. Whenever a man tells me how Spirit-filled he is, I always watch his actions to see if they back up his words. In my experience, they often don't.

I don't have any evidence of these theories other than observation and anecdotes, but I suspect they are true on at least some level. I don't find anything in the Bible that says women are more in tune with the persons of the Trinity, but it seems to me that because women are more attuned with the cycle of life, they perhaps have a better receiver to tune into God's spiritual radio waves.

Because of that lack of intimacy with God, I think men sometimes feel like their wives are more holy or spiritually mature, and thus men are reluctant to be spiritual leaders in the home. Women are then forced to pick up the ball as the role of spiritual leader and teacher.

Teacher

Women are often the first teachers of spirituality that young children have. I am always surprised at how many women either return to their faith or come to Christ after giving birth. The miracle of life must stir a primal instinct or understanding that intuitively prompts them to pass the knowledge of God's grace and mercy on to their offspring. Quite possibly, the very act of creating and growing new life within their body is so stunning in its complexity and majesty that women naturally (or even unconsciously) just know that at some level, an omnipotent Creator is involved. To create life within one's body, give birth, and hold a newborn baby and not develop faith in a Creator does not seem logical.

However, we men need to understand that when women are the only spiritual teachers in the home, the children get only a feminine vision of God and spirituality. This can be unappealing to boys and young men who yearn to know how and what a man feels about a relationship with God and what that looks like. Oftentimes when Mom is the only one who takes the kids to church, young boys become bored and would rather follow Dad's example of staying home.

Additionally, your wife and children need your spiritual leadership, as imperfect as it may be. God designated you as the "priest" in your home and holds you accountable for your actions or inactions in this area. If you step out in faith as a spiritual leader in your home, God will guide you in this area, and you will find greater fulfillment and satisfaction than you thought possible. Your wife and children are eager to follow your lead in this area.

Mentor

Women (and men) need healthy spiritual mentors. The key word here is *healthy*. I've seen many women led down the wrong path by seeking advice and wisdom from women (or men) who were either misguided or misinformed. The people we take guidance from directly determine the choices we make and thus where we end up in life.

While a woman's pastor should be one of those mentors, he or she cannot fulfill that role entirely. Being an effective mentor requires someone who cares about the person being mentored and invests in an intimate relationship with him or her. A woman needs another woman (or women), probably older and more spiritually mature, to help her fully grow in faith. In the model of Titus 2:3–5, she needs an older woman who has been through the trials and the despairs of life to help her glean wisdom and maturity—to teach her how to raise a family, love and support a husband, and develop a deep relationship with God.

Perhaps because of internal fears they possess, many women are reluctant or do not recognize their need for a mentor or other nurturing role models in their life. They feel it is fine for other women, but to admit that they need help or guidance would remove the cork from the bottle and release the "genie" of their fears, and then they might not be able to get the genie back in again. Also, perhaps the disconnectedness from family and community that most women experience now contributes to their reluctance to appear "needy." Teaching and counseling relationships used to happen more naturally than they do today. Perhaps women today can't find relationships they feel safe enough in to develop this kind of bond.

Fears

Many women I have spoken with say they struggle with a variety of fears. Fear of being an inadequate wife and mother, fear of not being considered beautiful, fear for their children, fear of being abandoned, fear of change, fear of loneliness, fear of failure, and fear of losing their man to another woman. Men have some of these fears too, but they are often more intensified in women. Women also have a great fear of rejection. Especially for those who have experienced rejection in their lives—by their fathers, by other girls and women, or by their lovers—rejection nearly becomes an obsession. When these women become adults, they are easily rejected. They tend to place too much emphasis on their husband's opinions of them instead of God's, giving their husband the power to emotionally reject them. Then when they feel slighted or rejected by their husband, their entire world falls apart, stifling them in many areas of life. Their fear of being rejected even debilitates them.

Many women also seem to feel guilty a lot. Most men I know do not suffer from this malady. Women even feel guilty about things they have no control over. This guilt causes them to make poor choices and limits their effectiveness in a variety of areas in their lives.

Many women, though, report that they are able to take these fears to God and focus on being grateful in order to overcome their fears. They need someone or something bigger than themselves or any of their problems to rely on in times when their fears become too great.

God says, "I will never reject you. I will never forsake you. I will love you unconditionally." But many women's perceptions of God are developed through their earthly father.

Her Father's Influence

Guys, you need to understand that a woman's father has a big influence in many areas of her life, but most especially in her view of her heavenly Father. If you can understand your wife's relationship with her father as a little girl and as a woman, and the power that relationship has, then you can begin to understand her relationship with God (and her relationship with you). This will help you to meet some of the needs she has in her spiritual walk—and she needs your support, strength, and leadership in this area.

The other day as my wife and I were driving, we listened to a radio program. The guest was Angela Thomas, the author of books such as *Do You Think I'm Beautiful?* and *My Single Mom Life*. Angela was describing her struggles as a single mom who was exhausted and overwhelmed by all the pressures of having four small children. She spoke about crying out to God and telling him she couldn't handle any more. God responded, she said, by paternally loving her, encouraging her, and calling her his "sweet baby girl."

I looked over at my wife, noticed she was crying, and asked her what was wrong. She said, "Never having had a father, I can't even imagine a loving heavenly Father calling me his sweet baby girl."

Since Angela is from the South—and I'm a little thickheaded—I responded, "Well, maybe that's a Southern thing."

Almost sobbing now, Suzanne said, "No, you call Kelsey your sweet baby girl all the time. It must be a dad thing!"

Later as she was relating that story to our daughter, even before she could get to the part about me calling her "sweet baby girl," Kelsey blurted out, "Daddy calls me his sweet baby girl!"

She then went on to tell Suzanne about a little note I gave her years ago. I don't even remember what it said—something about how you can truly live only when you take the focus off yourself and put it on others. But Kelsey apparently reads it every day and has it memorized. She keeps it on the bathroom counter in her apartment to look at every morning. But the most important part of the note was that it was signed, "I love you, sweet baby girl. Love, Daddy."

It humbles me to think that those few simple words from her father mean so much to her. And even more humbling is that her image and perspective of her heavenly Father will be so much more easily accessible due to the example I set in some small way as her earthly father.

Fathers have an incredible influence (positive or negative) on nearly every aspect of their daughters' lives. A common theme among women who did not have a father is the inability to trust a man and believe that she won't be abandoned again. Counting on and loving a man is a leap of faith, because for these women a permanent relationship with a man is theoretical.[1] And so women who suffer from father wounds tend to struggle with developing a close relationship with God as well. They cannot believe that he will not abandon them like their earthly father did. To admit to themselves that their earthly father loved them so little that he left them is difficult enough. Imagine how devastating it would be to think that the Creator of the universe wouldn't love them enough to stay.

Without a father around to provide a role model, healthy physical affection, and protection for her, a girl is left to the examples of masculinity she sees on television, the movies, and music videos—by all accounts, very poor options. She then transfers this image onto God. If her father and other older males in her life abandoned her, ignored her, or abused her, how can she possibly trust a heavenly Father? How can she risk fully giving her heart to someone who might once again leave her?

A father sets a huge example for his daughter regarding the qualities she looks for in men, the standards she maintains, and ultimately the qualities she attributes to God. He is the first man in her life and models how a man should treat a woman, how a man should act, and how a man shows healthy love and affection to a woman. He also sets the standard for how a daughter feels she deserves to be treated by men. He determines how a girl believes God should view her and treat her, and even how a girl feels about herself.

If a father shows his daughter love, respect, and appreciation for who she is, she will believe that about herself as a woman, no matter what anyone else thinks. How her father felt about her is how she will believe God feels about her.

I know one wonderful, competent woman who believes that God does not trust her. She is a successful single mom who owns her home and has a good job and great kids. Why would she believe she is incompetent and untrustworthy? Because she had a father who always criticized her and told her she was worthless. Even though intellectually she knows that's not true, it does not allow her heart to believe any different.

God's Daughter

All people, but especially women, have a lens or filter through which they see themselves. They get this perspective from their experiences in life, the way their caretakers treated them as a child, society's mores, and spiritual attacks on them. But the lens they see themselves through is rarely reality. For instance, many women believe in their hearts that they are physically unattractive, are overweight, or have any number of other negative characteristics. In their minds, this makes them less lovable, less worthy, less valuable as a person. The mirror they see themselves in is cracked or warped and reflects a distorted view or perception of them. In their hearts, they mourn their perceived lack of lovability and worth. They do not see themselves as God sees them—as beautiful daughters of Eve.

Women tend to look at their flaws through a magnifying glass instead of looking at themselves as a whole. Think of it this way. The area of the mountains where my wife likes to hike is beautiful. She often comes across gorgeous settings that take her breath away. But if she were to look at the pieces of the scene individually, she would notice that the ground is covered with animal scat, the pine needles are sticky with sap, the trees are covered with bugs, and the flowers are dirty and have bees around them. Individually, the scene is not so beautiful, but taken as a whole it is a magnificent example of God's beautiful creation.

The same goes for women. If they look only at their flaws and not the whole picture, they will never be satisfied and will never see God's magnificent creation—his culminating crown of creation. This self-misperception makes women susceptible to the affections (physical or verbal) of earthly men who would use them for their own self-gratification. It also prevents them from receiving the love and grace of a heavenly Father who wants them to know how glorious and spectacular he created them to be. With the power God has given a husband, who is one of the two most powerful men in a woman's life, is the ability to counteract these self-criticisms that a woman has by giving her honest compliments.

Most women are highly critical of themselves and have a deep desire for love and acceptance. This allows them to be easily swayed or even damaged by negative criticism. Author Steven James says, "Inside of every woman lives a needy little girl wanting to feel pretty, loved, secure. Expose her to her imperfections, toy with her desire to feel loved, rattle her sense of security, and you bring that needy little girl to the surface."[2]

Additionally, many young men complicate this cycle of woundedness by falling into the trap of feeling the need to "rescue" a damsel in distress. They see a broken young woman and instinctively try to rescue her. This is a behavior programmed into men—the need to be saviors and fix problems, especially of women and children. It's a good man who does this. Unfortunately, a husband can rarely fix the problems that are at the core of his wife's womanhood.

We all have wounds in our hearts or holes in our souls. Many people try to fill those empty spaces with drugs, alcohol, sex, power, or money to deaden the pain. But the truth is only God's love and forgiveness fill those wounds. Those wounds and the ways we try to soothe them also contribute to this distortion of how God perceives us. Many women believe that because of things they've done or mistakes they've made in the past, God will not or cannot forgive them. This is just not true, but guilt prevents them from allowing God's forgiveness to enter their hearts.

God can heal our wounds, but we must open them up and give them to him so that through his forgiveness, love, grace, and mercy, we can eventually forgive ourselves and even learn to love ourselves. And once we love ourselves, we can love others with even more grace, depth, and beauty.

Guys, you are the only man in the world who can counter-act any negative perceptions your wife's father or the world might have placed on her. As her husband, you are the only man besides her father whom God has granted the power to influence her in the core of her being. As a man, you know you have a fragile ego regarding your performance and your adequacy. Your wife's self-image regarding her beauty and value as a woman is just as fragile. When you love her, cherish her, respect her, and honor her, it can heal some of those wounds that damaged her heart. Please be conscious of that power and use it responsibly. If you use it poorly or not at all, it can cause even greater, irreversible damage.

Ladies, if you did not have a father growing up or had a poor role model for a father, it is vitally important that you look to your heavenly Father to fill that role in your life. He is a father who will always love you and care for you. His motives are always in your best interest. He never wishes harm on you. Without his love and healing, you are likely to continue making poor choices such as those modeled for you. Unfortunately, your husband cannot fulfill that role and those needs for you—only God can.

God loves you as a woman just the way he created you. You are a daughter of Eve, the magnificent culmination of his creation. It doesn't matter what you look like, how old you are, how much you weigh, how smart and accomplished you are, or how many mistakes you've made. He loves the inside of you—your heart, your entire being. That part deep down inside you that you never share with anyone else. He knows you even better than you know yourself—all of your imperfections and faults. Yet he still loves you unconditionally and willingly forgives all your sins and shortcomings. He always welcomes his children home with a Father's loving arms, no matter how far they've strayed.

Ask God for the fatherly love you should have gotten from your earthly father. Then allow him to heal the wounds of your heart so you can reap the rich blessings in life you deserve.

Fearfully and Wonderfully Made—Love the fact that God made her so different.

> Women often have a closer, deeper spiritual relationship with God than men do.
>
> Women are probably more willing to humble themselves before God than men are.
>
> A woman's earthly father plays a huge role in how she perceives her heavenly Father.
>
> A woman is generally the first spiritual teacher in her children's lives.
>
> A woman sees herself in the mirror as flawed, not as God does.

Get inside Her Head

> *This world is so frightening that I need an omnipotent God to rely upon.*
>
> *My father is disappointed in me, so how can God not be disappointed in me as well?*
>
> *I wish my husband would lead our family spiritually so I wouldn't have to.*
>
> *I hate the way I look—I'm unattractive and overweight.*

Words Have Meaning

Words That Heal

> "Honey, will you pray with me tonight?"
>
> "Kids, let's get ready for church!"

"God thinks you're awesome, and so do I."

"We'll get through this with God's help."

Words That Hurt

"Only weak people rely on religion as a crutch."

"All Christians are hypocrites."

"I wish you would quit bugging me to go to church."

"Would you lighten up? You don't need to be such a Goody Two-shoes all the time."

Girlfriends

The Sisterhood

What I expect from my male friends is that they are polite and clean. What I expect from my female friends is unconditional love, the ability to finish my sentences for me when I am sobbing, a complete and total willingness to pour their hearts out to me, and the ability to tell me why the meat thermometer isn't supposed to touch the bone.

Anna Quindlen, *Living Out Loud*

There is probably nothing more vital to a woman's satisfaction in life than to have one or more girlfriends. Having another woman to talk to, relate with, process information with, empathize with, and revel in her company is necessary to a woman's health and emotional well-being.

I heard Dr. James Dobson say something very profound on his radio show once. He referred back to the days when women used to have a stronger bond and community with each other. Everything they did—washing clothes, preparing meals, raising kids—they did together. Today there is an absence of these kinds of powerful, nurturing relationships that women need.

Dr. Dobson stated that when a husband comes home from work, the wife often looks to him to fulfill needs created by the lack of female relationships. These needs are critical to her life, but a man cannot fill them. One woman said, "Having women in my life is definitely important and as necessary to my overall serenity as air! They are the ones I trust to understand the journey and who may be the only gender that could understand why the books I talk about are romantic."

Women need girlfriends to help satisfy the need that a man cannot fill. While a man quickly runs out of words, a girlfriend can actively listen and participate in the conversation on her level. A girlfriend will be involved in the conversation, laugh, cry, be empathetic, offer assistance, and be supportive. One of Suzanne's co-workers once told me, "We can laugh at the silly things, talk over a cup of coffee, go to lunch, and shop till we drop." Girlfriends are a woman's extended family. A woman's girlfriends help keep her emotionally stable, psychologically balanced and content, and physically healthy.

But there are other, even better reasons why your wife should have girlfriends.

Shopping

For women, shopping is today's equivalent of gathering roots and berries. For most of the history of the world, women came together to do a variety of activities. This communal behavior included gathering food, cooking, and making necessities such as blankets and clothing. Women got together to share woes, watch each other's kids, swap stories, and be productive. They learned from one another, with young girls interfacing directly with older female role models. Today, with families strung out across the country, women rely on friends, and increasingly the Internet, for connectedness. Because women are so relational, they need other women who can understand their needs and concerns.

I've observed this need for female bonding up close and personal in our home. My daughter, much like my wife, seems to relate better to males than females and has a hard time making girlfriends. But she has a yearning for female companionship that keeps her searching for a friend who can sit and chat, shop, and cry with her. I have also noted a yearning she has to learn from older females. She has been frustrated in her attempts to get older women to nurture and advise her. Perhaps because of this, my wife and daughter are bonded closely, but I sense each longs deeply for other, outside associations.

Guys, encourage your wife to have healthy girlfriends. If nothing else, it gives her someone besides you to go shopping with. That way you do not have to go from store to store looking at "cute" shoes all day. (Do men have cute shoes? What would that look like?) And how are you supposed to answer that inevitable question, "How does this look on me?" There's no good answer. That question only leads down a slippery path laden with quicksand, tangled and prickly undergrowth, and poisonous vipers. Even the most adventurous and foolhardy man treads carefully down that dark and lonely path of no return. The average guy, if quick on his feet, just nods and smiles. Since she ignores what you say about clothes anyway, it just reinforces her opinion that you are clueless about fashion and thus lowers her expectations of you in this area. It can be a dangerous strategy (you need to have a vague but unoffending response ready if she forces you to talk), but it's the best one I've found to navigate these shark-infested waters.

And there's not anything much more embarrassing than standing around looking dim-witted outside the ladies' dressing room, holding an armful of women's unmentionables. I made the mistake of being along once when my wife and daughter went shopping for bras. I kid you not, it was *the* most grueling, excruciatingly painful experience of my life. After eight hours of trying on every bra in the store, they were just getting ramped up. They flung discarded bras out of the dressing rooms so fast and furious that some of them landed on my head and shoulders. Besides feeling like a pervert for standing around in the women's underwear section all day, I could have read *War and Peace* in the time it took them to find a bra, had I not been so faint from hunger.

Since I had already memorized every square foot of merchandise in the store by this time, I started reading the employee rules on the bulletin board and sighing loudly and dramatically every few minutes. The women who worked in the store just looked at me with disdain, and the male employees gave me looks of pity while scurrying about their business so as not to get inadvertently sucked into an estrogen vortex. They knew a desperate guy when they saw one, and even though sympathetic, they didn't want anything to do with me.

I'm not sure why, but I can work out at the gym, go for a long bike ride in the mountains, and swim laps and still not be as exhausted as I am after shopping for an hour. Women are brutal when they shop. As near as I can tell, women who are focused on shopping see nonrelated men as inanimate objects to be pushed aside without acknowledgment if they are in the way, and related men to be handy pack mules that they don't even feel obligated to feed and water every so often.

There's something about standing around on those cold, hard floors while being pushed around by every woman intent on getting a bargain that is just plain draining. I have been bumped, elbowed, stepped on, and hissed at during sales events—and that was at a Christian bazaar. One lady looked at me like, "You don't belong here, Junior, so get out of the way before someone gets hurt!" It's like a combat zone out there—every so often a strange woman jumps out from behind a counter and sprays you in the eyes with some kind of toxic gas labeled "perfume." High heels puncture your toe as a woman dashes past you to grab the last Donna Karan suit reduced to 70 percent. Saleswomen are trained to ignore you except when they deftly swipe the credit card out of your hand like an experienced pickpocket, all the while chatting with your wife like a long-lost friend.

Some stores provide a "man chair" outside the women's dressing room, for which I am truly grateful. It's generally a wobbly, hard, metal folding chair. Unfortunately, if you don't move every so often, the women start piling discarded clothes on you like a clothing rack. I want to find a store that provides a separate air-conditioned room with a soft leather recliner, a TV turned to a sports channel, snacks, and ice-cold beverages for men whose women are trying on outfits. Since women wear clothes for other women, not men, a saleslady should patiently stand outside the dressing room door and answer that dreaded question about how she looks in each outfit. That would be my idea of shopping. But I digress. . . .

Okay, I'm poking fun at women's love of shopping, but the truth is that it is a talent and requires specific skills that many men lack. In fact, there are logical reasons that women shop longer than men do. Women take in and retain much more information when they walk into a room. Women have a 360-degree perspective on life and, when shopping, evaluate products and services by how they fit into that bigger picture. Women are interactive in their shopping style and are more likely to try on, test, and sample products before purchasing, and they tend to imagine how they will interact afterward with the products in their daily lives. Because they are relational, women interact more with sales associates and get more peer and expert opinions for their purchases than men.[1] Hence, women have a need for a longer and more fulfilling shopping experience.

Talking

Does anyone doubt that women talk more than men do? A woman speaks about twenty to thirty thousand words each day, compared to a measly ten thousand words spoken by the average man—and that's counting grunts and mutters. Plus, men typically speak more in public and less in private, while women are just the opposite. Therefore, logically, men cannot possibly compete with women in the area of conversation. This is where girlfriends come in handy. One woman said it like this: "My husband is my best friend, but my girlfriend knows me better than my husband and she is a woman, so she can understand 'woman' things better than my husband does." Seems simple enough to me.

Sometimes on a Saturday my wife will be getting ready to go shopping or hiking or out to lunch with her friends. (I don't know exactly what "lunch" means, but they must eat slowly because it always takes a long time.) She will be all in a dither and will start warming up her conversation skills on me. Of course, I am counting the minutes until she leaves and I can watch the ball game in peace and quiet. And because female time is different than male time, her girlfriends will inevitably be late, causing me even greater duress.

I've observed my wife or daughter when they haven't been around each other or one of their friends for a while. When they get together, they each start talking so fast they can hardly understand one another. The words and gestures and emotions are spilling out so fast that they can't control them. I've seen women who were good friends just start bawling under those circumstances. The need to talk is so powerful that they're overwhelmed.

I've also noticed that women who have not seen each other for a while will huddle together and get away by themselves for a period of time—usually in the kitchen. When friends come to visit, that is usually the first place the women head off to. After they have sated their craving for female bonding, they are able to be more convivial in a group of mixed company.

One woman from a workshop expressed her need to talk this way:

> I get together with a group of ladies to scrapbook, and it is always the same. We drag all of our billions of photos and stickers and paper to one house where there are no husbands or kids in sight! We absolutely love to scrapbook, but I think that the scrapbooking is mostly just a cover for girlfriend time.
>
> As a mom, you sometimes feel the need to give a reasonable excuse to have "girlfriend" time. We use scrapbooking because it's something for our family. But really it's for us. We need a break. We need time to laugh about the things our kids did and the erratic things we did because we had to ask our husbands to take the trash out fifty-seven times! Sometimes I get in the mood to just talk about random stuff that doesn't really have any point at all besides talking, where one topic runs into the other until you can't even remember what you started talking about.

Talking apparently leads into one other area where girl-friends come in handy—the bathroom.

The Bathroom

Lastly, girlfriends are good for your wife because it gives her someone to go to the bathroom with. One of the great mysteries of life is why women feel compelled to go to the bathroom together. Frankly, I don't know what goes on in there, but again, it seems like a female bonding ritual that all women fall prey to. I'm sure all kinds of mysterious rituals and ceremonies take place in the bathroom. I can honestly say that in my entire life I have never asked another man to accompany me to the restroom. That would be a good way to get punched in the nose.

Men are quite curious as to what the inside of a female restroom looks like, though. We envision these exotic palaces with all kinds of elegant fixtures, pillows, and opulent furniture overlaid with the swirling scent of spices and perfumes—sort of a sultan's harem quarters. Furnished with plush velvet "fainting" couches and stocked with warm hand towels, it is a place for women to be pampered and rejuvenated before coming back out into the harsh light of reality. Why else would they be in there so long?

I'm sure reality is much more disillusioning, but we prefer to maintain our fantasies.

Guys, your wife needs healthy girlfriends in her life, especially if you have young children. It's important that you make sure she gets alone time with her girlfriends. It will make her healthier, happier, and more willing to meet your needs—definitely a good trade-off from my perspective. And since relationships are important to women, make an effort to get to know the husbands of her girlfriends. Spending time together with other couples is fun and invigorating to your relationship. It's either that or going shopping.

Fearfully and Wonderfully Made—Love the fact that God made her so different.

Women process information and emotions by talking with other women.

Women like to talk.

Women need the company of other women.

A woman can share all her internal complexities and needs with a girlfriend.

Girlfriends are like sisters, only better.

Get inside Her Head

No one can understand what I'm feeling except my best friend.

I am so lonely without any friends or family around.

How come my husband won't open up and share with me like my girlfriends?

I can't wait to go shopping with my friend!

Words Have Meaning

Words That Heal

"I'll watch the kids; why don't you go have lunch with your girlfriends?"

"Hey, why don't you see if your friend and her husband want to get together this weekend?"

"That's exciting! Why don't you call Sally and share it with her?"

"I'm glad you have such good friends."

Words That Hurt

"I can't stand your girlfriend."

"Your friend is a bad influence on you."

"You listen to your girlfriends more than you do me."

"This is a good career opportunity for me. You'll make new friends."

Wrap-Up

What if God didn't design marriage to be "easier"?
What if God had an end in mind that went beyond
our happiness, our comfort, and our desire to be
infatuated and happy as if the world were a perfect
place?

Gary Thomas, *Sacred Marriage*

One of the greatest fallacies we buy into is that there is the "perfect" person out there just waiting to make us happy for the rest of our lives if we can only find them. Many of us spend our entire lives, including our marriages, dreaming of a person who would complete our life and make us happy and content. I'm convinced that person doesn't exist and that our marriage is more about what we make it than any predestined or preordained match made in heaven. The myth of the "soul mate" has been foisted upon men and women like bad cake at a wedding.

Another error that people buy into is the illusion that love means the absence of conflict. Just as people want to believe that pain and sadness should be avoided at all costs, they believe that love means no conflict.[1]

If you believe that the right person will come along and make you happy, you are deluded. You, not other people, are responsible for your own happiness. Every relationship, especially one of love, is painful and often difficult. That's why it is worthwhile. With the beauty and fragrance of a rose come the thorns that scratch and sometimes draw blood. Going through the struggles of life together brings you closer and bonds you deeper. Those relationships without conflict and pain are dead, cold, and passionless. I say rejoice in your conflicts because it means your marriage is alive and growing!

One of the ways we deal with conflict is through effective communication. Some people will have read this book and say that I forgot to include the most important aspect of a healthy marriage—communication. Communication *is* important—very important—to any relationship, especially marriage. In fact, the way you speak to each other actually determines the quality of your marriage. If you speak to each other in a respectful, loving, affirming manner, then those feelings will follow and be ingrained in your relationship. But if you speak words of spite, contempt, and anger, then those feelings will rule, and eventually destroy, your relationship.

The truth is that this entire book is about communication. It is about understanding the language of your spouse in order to satisfy his or her needs. However, communication is not the problem in most marriages. Dr. Laura Schlessinger says, "I don't think that many marriages are stuck on communication problems, whatever they are. I think most marriages are stuck on people needing or hurting so much (from their childhoods, primarily) that they forget to or resist giving love."[2] If that is true, then what does make the difference between a healthy marriage relationship and a destructive one?

Our daughter recently mentioned to my wife that she wanted a love like we have, that we still acted like we were on our honeymoon. I don't know whose house she's been living in for the past twenty years, but I don't often feel like we're still honeymooners. But in hindsight, perhaps because my wife and I still frequently hold hands, hug and kiss, and even dance together in the living room, our daughter feels we have a great love. We like to travel together, and we enjoy each other's company (she's probably the only one who could put up with me). We speak respectfully to each other and try to be cheerleaders for one another. Our actions and words not only direct our feelings but also signify to others our love and passion for one another. In short, we are good friends. That friendship fuels our love for one another and carries us through those rough spots when one of us is feeling disagreeable or fed up with the other.

Many young couples today are frustrated with each other and their marriage because neither partner knows how to relate to the other. No one has ever taught them the fundamentals of building an intimate relationship, so they are starting from scratch, guessing at how a marriage works. This confusion causes arguments and disagreements. According to Robert Lewis and William Hendricks, "What these young people don't realize is that *behind much of their quarrels and dysfunction and anger is what they don't know*, not *who they're married to*."[3] This lack of taught communication skills (which were often never modeled for them in their parents' marriages) creates tension and prevents intimacy in a relationship.

But perhaps of more importance than even communication in a marriage is love—love that is not a feeling or an emotion, but one that is a verb, an action word. If we take loving *actions* in our relationships, the *feelings* of love will follow. There's an old adage that thoughts become actions and actions become feelings. Your attitude is everything.

Noted psychologist Erich Fromm calls this kind of love an "art," a learned and practiced skill just like painting, carpentry, or music.[4] As he says, the problem with most people is that of *being loved*, rather than that of *loving*, or one's capacity to love.[5] Most people are more concerned about how to be loved than how they can give love. They are more concerned with having *their* needs met than meeting the needs of their spouse.

The practice of any art has certain general requirements, whether it is the art of carpentry, medicine, or love. First, the practice of an art requires *discipline*. Without the discipline to practice and memorize, a musician could never become adept at playing the piano, an artist could never learn to paint, and a doctor could never learn to heal people. Without discipline, we are easily swayed into wallowing in our own narcissistic needs rather than focusing on the needs of our spouse.

Concentration is also vital to the mastery of an art. Concentration is almost a lost ability in today's world of distractions, noises, and multitasking. Lack of concentration also keeps us from focusing on lifting up others and allows us to slip back into our own hazy miasma of self-gratification.

Next, the mastery of an art requires *patience*. Anyone who has ever tried to master an art knows patience is necessary if they want to achieve anything. And the art of marriage takes patience. Unfortunately, our whole world today is focused on the opposite of patience: quickness. Machines get us from one place to another faster and faster. I want my fast food seconds after I order it. I don't particularly want to wait until my wife is sufficiently turned on before I have my sexual needs gratified, and I definitely don't want to wait until I've worked at something twenty years before I receive the benefits of my labor.

Finally, a high level of *concern* is a necessary condition to master any art form. If something is not very important to us, we will never spend the time and energy required to become adept at it.[6]

Of course, we must understand that we do not learn an art directly or immediately. We must learn many seemingly disconnected (and even unrelated) skills before we can begin to learn the art itself. For instance, an apprentice carpenter must learn (over a period of years) to choose the wood, measure it, and cut it properly before he is ever allowed to start creating a beautiful staircase or bookcase. An apprentice violinist plays scales, learns to read music, learns music theory, and practices untold hours before ever playing a recital. Medical students spend years in school and under the tutelage of older, more experienced doctors before being allowed to practice medicine.

With regard to the art of loving, we must begin by practicing discipline, concentration, and patience throughout every phase and aspect of our lives.[7] And without concern, we never care enough to go to the trouble of mastering all of these traits. If we want to be adept at the "art of love," we must first become proficient at a variety of other skills such as forgiveness, self-sacrifice, passion, and an altruistic regard for the fulfillment of our partner's needs and desires.

Fromm also proposes that there are certain elements common to all forms of love, including care, responsibility, respect, and knowledge. Without active *care* and concern, there can be no love. Understand that this means physically doing the acts necessary to convey a loving, caring attitude. *Responsibility* often denotes a form of duty today, but in truth it is a voluntary act. To be responsible is to be able and ready to respond, specifically to the needs of those you love. Responsibility might easily deteriorate into domination and possessiveness were it not for the third component of love, *respect*. Respect means that you value your spouse as worthy of your love. Finally, to respect someone requires that you know them. Care and responsibility would be blind if not guided by *knowledge*, and knowledge would be empty without concern or care.[8]

Did Adam love Eve? Perhaps, but maybe he really didn't understand the meaning of the word, or he wouldn't have tried to blame Eve in the Garden of Eden when God confronted them about eating from the tree of the knowledge of good and evil. True love would have prompted Adam to have taken the blame for Eve's actions—to have stood in front of her and protected her. True love sacrifices itself for another. True love stays despite difficulties or hardships. True love works to meet the needs (modes and moods) of the other with no expectations in return. True love is sacrificial, but not with a sense of martyrdom. It is a *wanting* to give, not an obligatory or compulsive sense of "should" or "must." It cannot be a narcissistic love but one that is freely and generously given without restrictions or conditions.

Two-thirds of the divorces in this country are filed by women. The biggest reason given is that they are not emotionally fulfilled. I'm not criticizing women, and I know men are more than responsible for their fair share of divorces, but that particular reason strikes me as more of a selfish love than a giving one. Frankly, if my wife had had that attitude over the years, she would have had grounds for divorce many times. Her commitment and perseverance allowed our relationship (and me) to grow and mature until I was better able to meet her needs.

Perhaps it is unrealistic to expect this kind of selflessness in a culture that demands total fulfillment and self-satisfaction out of every relationship, or quickly abandons a relationship for one more attractive. Of course, the same problems follow and nag the subsequent relationship as well, because it is not about having your needs met but about meeting the needs of your spouse. Love is about giving, not receiving.

Having a successful marriage is not about finding the perfect person to marry, although that is what many people believe. It is about loving someone in a forgiving, Christlike manner. The Bible illustrates this agape-type love in many stories, ranging from Hosea, who continued to love and take back his adulterous wife, to Joseph, who forgave his brothers for selling him into slavery. In my experience, love requires nearly constant forgiveness.

Love also requires us to have a great deal of faith. We must have faith in our spouse in order to truly love them. We must have faith in the reliability and unchangeability of their fundamental attitudes and character, of the core of their personality, and of their love toward us.[9] Without that faith, we will fail to have a foundation on which to build trust and love. As Fromm so eloquently puts it, "To love means to commit oneself without guarantee, to give oneself completely in hope that our love will produce love in the loved person. Love is an act of faith, and whoever is of little faith is also of little love."[10]

It's not that marriage cannot be happy and joyous. A good marriage has more joy and satisfaction than any other relationship in life. But long-term relationships require dedicated work, perseverance, commitment, forgiveness, and patience. As James 1:12 says, we must endure the trials and challenges so that we can experience the true joy and love that God has promised.

When we talk about a "labor of love," we are talking about the fact that being in love—loving someone (including ourselves)—takes effort and work. Fromm says, "Love and labor are inseparable. One loves that for which one labors, and one labors for that which one loves."[11] Love is essentially an act of the will, a decision to commit your life to that of another person.[12] The joy in a relationship comes precisely because of the struggles a couple has overcome. The degree to which we persevere through adversity is the degree of satisfaction we will receive in return.

Love also requires courage. To be loved, and to love, requires the courage to judge certain values as of ultimate concern— and to take the jump and stake everything on those values.[13]

Most of all, true love requires sacrifice.

As we look for love that fills the desires of our hearts, let us always remember that we get what we give. If we desire sacrificial love, we must give sacrificial love. If we desire unconditional love, we must give unconditional love. If we desire forgiveness, we must extend forgiveness. If we crave passion, we must be passionate.

Love is a choice. If we choose to love, we will be loved in return. God chooses to love us despite our imperfections. This in turn should inspire us to extend the same grace to the person we have chosen to spend our lives with and to be the mother or father of our children. If that is not possible, perhaps we should have made a better choice to begin with.

Two last bits of advice for a happy marriage. First, laugh together every day. Laughter releases chemicals (natural narcotics) into your bloodstream, causing you to feel joy and pleasure and reducing stress. My marriage is always so much better when Suzanne and I laugh together. Laughter makes so many other things seem trivial. It also helps heal wounds and grievances.

Second, try new things together—frequently. Often the novelty of marriage and romance wears off as people get into the daily grind and routine of life. Trying new and exciting things together stimulates your relationship, causes you to grow together, and develops intimacy. My marriage has been rejuvenated in recent years by my wife's and my taking trips together and entering into new relationships, situations, and circumstances in which we have never found ourselves before.

Today my wife and I both look forward to the next twenty-seven years of marriage even more than we did the first twenty-seven. Laugh together and try new adventures together, and you will too. Remember, love isn't about you—it's about the one you love.

May God's blessings be on your marriage and on your lives. *Vaya con Dios.*

Notes

Introduction

1. Harville Hendrix, *Getting the Love You Want* (New York: Henry Holt & Co., 1988), 41.
2. Ibid., chapters 2–4.
3. Dr. Les Parrott and Dr. Leslie Parrott, *Saving Your Marriage Before It Starts* (Grand Rapids: Zondervan, 1995), 28.
4. Bill and Pam Farrel, *Men Are Like Waffles—Women Are Like Spaghetti* (Eugene, OR: Harvest House Publishers, 2001).
5. Helen Fisher, *The First Sex* (New York: Ballantine, 1999), 5–6.
6. Hendrix, *Getting the Love You Want*, 55.
7. Ibid., xiv.

Men's Mode #1 Amorous

1. Peggy Vaughan, *Monogamy Myth* (New York: Newmarket Press, 2003), 7.
2. "Infidelity Statistics," Infidelity Facts, 2006, http://www.infidelityfacts.com/infidelity-statistics.html.
3. William Glasser, MD, and Carleen Glasser, *Getting Together and Staying Together* (New York: HarperCollins, 2000), 30.
4. Stephen Arterburn, Fred Stoecker, and Mike Yorkey, *Every Man's Battle* (Colorado Springs: WaterBrook Press, 2000), 63.
5. Don Robertson, *The Greatest Thing Since Sliced Bread* (New York: G. P. Putnam & Sons, 1965), 35.
6. Shaunti Feldhahn, *For Women Only: What You Need to Know about the Inner Lives of Men* (Sisters, OR: Multnomah Publishers, 2004), 92.
7. Ibid., 92–93.

Men's Mode #2 Work

1. Parrott and Parrott, *Saving Your Marriage*, 105.

Men's Mode #5 Protector

1. Wikipedia, "Have Gun Will Travel," July 21, 2009, http://en.wikipedia.org/wiki/Have_Gun_-_Will_Travel.
2. Ibid.
3. Will Davis, *Pray Big for Your Marriage* (Grand Rapids: Revell, 2008), 31.
4. John Connolly, *The Unquiet* (New York: Pocket Star Books, 2007), 320–21.
5. Much of his section was excerpted from David McLaughlin's teachings in his seminar "The Role of the Man." David has been giving these workshops to men around the country for the past twenty-five years, and God has used him to change the lives of many men for the better. Used with permission.

Men's Mode #6 Connection with God

1. Connolly, *The Unquiet*, 504.

Women's Mood #3 Playful

1. Quoted in Lisa Johnson and Andrea Learned, *Don't Think Pink* (New York: AMACOM, 2004), 10.

Women's Mood #4 Nurturing

1. Science Daily, "Brain Imaging Shows How Men and Women Cope Differently Under Stress," November 20, 2007, http://www.sciencedaily.com/releases/2007/11/071119170133.htm.
2. Dr. Laura Schlessinger, *The Proper Care and Feeding of Marriage* (New York: HarperCollins, 2007), 54.
3. Robert Lewis and William Hendricks, *Rocking the Roles* (Colorado Springs: Navpress, 1998), 57.

Women's Mood #5 Cycle

1. US Department of Health and Human Services, "Menstruation and the Menstrual Cycle," April 1, 2007, http://www.womenshealth.gov/faq/menstru.htm#b.
2. Women's Health Information, "Menstrual Cycles: What Really Happens in Those 28 Days?!" Feminist's Women's Health Center, May 20, 2009, http://www.fwhc.org/health/moon.htm.
3. Medline Plus, "Painful Menstrual Periods," November 9, 2007, http://www.nlm.nih.gov/medlineplus/ency/article/003150.htm.
4. Ibid.
5. Jean Lush, *Emotional Phases of a Woman's Life* (Grand Rapids: Revell, 1990).

6. Dr. Daniel Amen, "Images of PMS," November, 2, 2008, http://www.amen clinics.com/bp/atlas/ch10.php.
7. Ibid.
8. Ibid.

Women's Mood #6 Spiritual

1. Victoria Secunda, *Women and Their Fathers: The Sexual and Romantic Impact of the First Man in Your Life* (New York: Delacorte Press, 1992), 211.
2. Steven James, *The Rook* (Grand Rapids: Revell, 2008), 366–67.

Women's Mood #7 Girlfriend

1. Johnson and Learned, *Don't Think Pink*, 18.

Wrap-Up

1. Erich Fromm, *The Art of Loving* (New York: Harper & Row, 1956), 95.
2. Schlessinger, *Proper Care*, 103.
3. Lewis and Hendricks, *Rocking the Roles*, 212 (italics in the original).
4. Fromm, *The Art of Loving*, 5.
5. Ibid., 1.
6. Ibid., 100–101.
7. Ibid., 102.
8. Ibid., 25–27.
9. Ibid., 114.
10. Ibid., 118.
11. Ibid., 26.
12. Ibid., 52.
13. Ibid., 117.

Bestselling author and speaker **Rick Johnson** founded Better Dads, a fathering skills program based on the urgent need to empower men to lead and serve in their families and communities. Rick's books have expanded his ministry to include influencing the whole family, with life-changing insights for men and women on parenting, marriage, and personal growth. He is a sought-after speaker at many large conferences across the United States and Canada and is a popular keynote speaker at men's and women's retreats and conferences on parenting and marriage. Additionally, Rick is a nationally recognized expert in several areas, including the effects of fatherlessness, and has been asked to teach papers at various educational venues.

To find out more about Rick Johnson, his books, and the Better Dads ministry, or to schedule workshops, seminars, or speaking engagements, please visit www.betterdads.net.

INSPIRE YOUR MAN TO GREATNESS

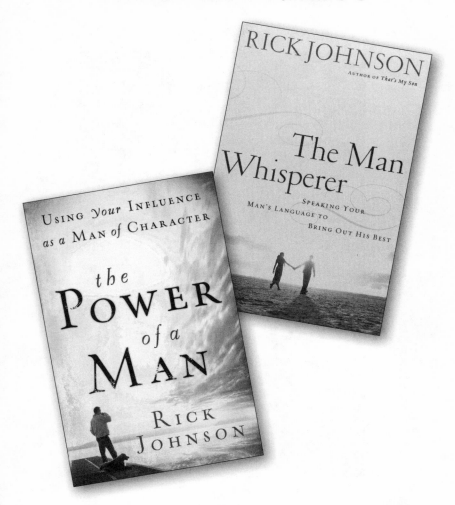

Discover how you can bring out the best in your man
with these great resources.

DON'T MISS THESE
OTHER GREAT TITLES

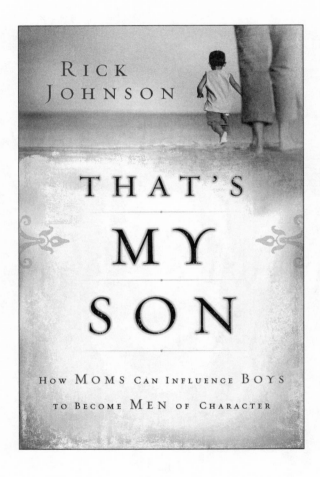

A mother's imprint on her son lasts forever.

 Revell
a division of Baker Publishing Group
www.RevellBooks.com

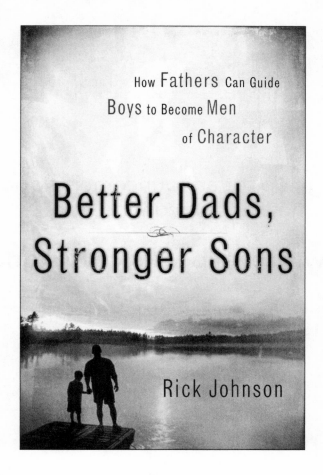